HAIL TO RFK!

35 Seasons of Redskins Memories

By John Keim, Rick Snider and David Elfin

Photos by Arnie Sachs and the staff of Consolidated News Photo, Joe Silverman and Ranny Routt

Copyright 1996

21st Century Online Publishing Inc.
http:choicemall.com/dc/dc177-01

To order additional copies, call 1-800-333-5588

To my wife Lisa and daughters Megan and Katelyn for their love and support.

— Rick Snider

To my father, Mel, who nurtured my obsession with the Redskins, and to my wife Loretta, who allows it to thrive.

— David Elfin

To my wife Kerry, whose support and encouragement sustain me, and to my son Matthew, whose presence inspires me.

— John Keim

Acknowledgments

The authors would like to thank Progressive Publishing Group, Inc., graphic designer Patricia Nieves, photographers Joe Silverman, Arnie Sachs and the staff of Consolidated News Photo and Dick Burke for providing photos by the late Ranny Routt, the public relations staff of the Washington Redskins, Washington Times sports editor Gary Hopkins, Washington Times copy editor Dick Heller and Journal sports editor Paul Bergeron for their contributions and support of the book.

Table of Contents

RFK THROUGH THE YEARS

RFK Through The Years

The Beatles rocked there. The Stones rolled there. It has hosted the Olympics and the World Cup. It has been home to Senators and Diplomats. They've played a baseball All-Star Game and a bowl game there.

But as Robert F. Kennedy Stadium celebrates its 35th anniversary this fall, the place is best known for one thing: it's the home of the NFL's Washington Redskins.

The club plans to move into its new, 78,000-seat, luxury-boxed digs five miles up the road in Landover, Md. sometime in 1997, but RFK will always belong to the Redskins and the Redskins to RFK.

"The team can move to the new stadium, but RFK will always be the Redskins' home to me," said linebacker Monte Coleman, who played in a club-record 216 games from 1979-94.

Quarterback Joe Theismann, a Redskin from 1974-85, couldn't agree more.

"Any player who came to RFK knew he wasn't just playing the Redskins," Theismann said. "He had to deal with a whole bunch of other people, 55,000-plus. That place would rock and roll, man. When I stepped on the field at RFK, it was just like sitting down in a big easy chair in my living room because I had my family around me."

If you were part of the Dallas Cowboys' family, you hated RFK. The Cowboys were whipped by the Redskins at RFK in the 1972 and 1982 NFC Championship Games. The movable lower stands shook those afternoons as if part of the soundstage for the film "Earthquake." The hated visitors from Texas never had a chance. And RFK's atmosphere was the same on a December afternoon in 1992 when the Cowboys visited en route to the first of their back-to-back Super Bowl titles.

"I hated RFK when I was with Dallas," said center John Gesek, who played his final two seasons with Washington. "The field was slippery and it was so loud."

The noise helped cost the Cowboys in that 1992 game.

"We were backed up in our end," Gesek remembered. "[Quarterback] Troy [Aikman] had to call an audible at the line and the fans in the end zone were so loud, I don't think all of our guys heard him."

Redskins backup defensive tackle Jason Buck knocked the ball from Aikman's grasp and after a wild chase for the ball, Washington safety Danny Copeland came up with it in the end zone for the touchdown which gave the Redskins a thrilling 20-17 victory. It would prove to be the last at RFK for Washington's Hall of Fame coach Joe Gibbs, who retired the following March.

"When you walk into that stadium it's one of the greatest feelings in pro sports," Gibbs said during his July 1996 Hall of Fame induction. "Yeah, it was a crummy stadium with crud hanging off it. And the fans are right on top of everybody. But I'll tell you this, when people came in there, it was hard to beat us. Part of what's going on up here today belongs to you [the fans]."

It may be hard to believe for those who only knew an aging RFK in the 1980s and 1990s, but when the building, then known as District of Columbia Stadium, opened on Oct. 1, 1961, it was state of the art. Its cantilevered roof was the first in an American stadium.

"Magnificent," raved The Washington Post, which referred to the stadium's "form-fitting, theater-type seats." More than 13,000 of those seats went unfilled that Sunday afternoon as the Redskins blew a 21-7 lead and lost to the New York Giants, 24-21. The crowd of 36,767 was still bigger than the capacity at old Griffith Stadium and was thus the largest ever to see a sporting event in Washington.

The defeat was typical for the Redskins of that era. Washington had endured five straight losing seasons and would finish under .500 during its first five years at its new home at East Capitol and 22nd Streets N.E. In fact, the Redskins would lose their first six games at D.C. Stadium en route to a 1-12-1 season. But halfback Dick James made that first home victory memorable by rushing for a team-record four touchdowns against Dallas.

The stadium was built by the District government on federal land. The construction, which took just 15 months and cost $24 million (almost three times the projected budget from 1958), began during the Eisenhower administration. However, by the time the stadium opened, John Kennedy was in the Oval Office.

The Redskins had never had a black player, a fact the NAACP protested outside the stadium the day it opened. Owner George Preston Marshall didn't want to offend his millions of Southern fans. The Redskins owned the South in the era when radio – not national television – ruled and the Atlanta Falcons, Carolina Panthers, New Orleans Saints, Miami Dolphins and Tampa Bay Buccaneers didn't exist.

Kennedy wasn't eager to enter the civil rights fray, but this was an easy fight. Secretary of the Interior Stewart Udall told Marshall his team would have to find another stadium if it didn't integrate. Before the year was out, Marshall had traded for Cleveland halfback Bobby Mitchell, the first great player in the Redskins' new home.

"My whole life is RFK," said Mitchell, now the Redskins assistant general manager. "They could name the new stadium after me and it wouldn't take its place."

In 1969, D.C. Stadium was renamed for Robert F. Kennedy, the senator and attorney general who had been assassinated the year before while running for President. That same year, the baseball Senators - who would move to Texas in 1971 after a dramatic final forfeit when the crowd rushed the field before the final out - would host the All-Star Game and have the only winning season of their 10 in the stadium. Hall of Famer Ted Williams was their manager and huge Frank Howard their slugger.

In that same memorable year, 1969, Williams' Redskins counterpart, the legendary Vince Lombardi, arrived to coach the team to its first winning season since 1955. Lombardi died of cancer the following year, but the Redskins rose to even greater glory under successors George Allen (40-10-1 at RFK from 1971-77) and Joe Gibbs (78-24 at RFK from 1981-92). The Redskins sold out their final 31 seasons at RFK, but not just because the team won most of the time.

"Our fans are intelligent," said current Redskins general manager Charley Casserly. "They know when to cheer. They don't need to be prompted by a scoreboard. It's a very loud stadium. The band playing 'Hail To The Redskins' is one of the great moments in pro football. You get goosebumps. Denver, Kansas City and Giants Stadium are loud too, but RFK is unique.

Defensive end Charles Mann, who played 11 of his 12 NFL seasons at RFK, loved playing there during the glory days of the 1980s.

"We were just loved and admired like you wouldn't believe," Mann said. "They appreciated the people behind the uniforms. Getting in and out of RFK was a chore. People couldn't get even tickets from scalpers in the parking lots. I remember how the fans rocked the stands. This is part of the mystique of RFK and the Redskins. They're playing a tune we had heard a bunch, but none of us would want them to change because it was part of who we were. You talk about home-field advantage. Coach Gibbs brainwashed you into being concerned about the team you were about to face, but you always felt pretty good when you were playing at RFK. When push came to shove, we would get our fans involved."

Mark Moseley, the Redskins' kicker from 1974-86 and their all-time leading scorer, wasn't joking when he said he would like to be buried at RFK. That's how much their stadium meant to the Redskins.

That was especially true for Mitchell, who has spent as many Sundays at RFK as anyone. "This might sound crazy, but when I go through those darn chutes coming up to the dugout, I hear so many things," said Mitchell. "I hear all the things that went on there with me, every game, all the sadness, all the great fun. It all happens when I go through the dug out. I see people I used to be with, who used to be standing there, used to be talking there. I can't explain it other than to say it's there."

RFK will still be there after the Redskins leave. Stadium executive director Jim Dalrymple said between soccer, college football and concerts, the facility will still be busy and profitable. But it won't be the same without the Redskins. Or they without RFK.

photo by Arnie Sachs and the staff of Consolidated News Photo

RFK Stadium — Thanks for all the memories

By Sam Huff

I remember the first game ever at D.C. Stadium. I was with the visiting New York Giants for the third game of the 1961 season. We were used to playing in old baseball stadiums around the country like Yankee Stadium and Griffith Stadium. Now we had some place new and exciting. The Redskins would finish 1-12-1 that season, but they hit an emotional high for the opener and almost beat us as the Giants escaped 24-21.

Three years later, I was traded to the Washington Redskins and RFK Stadium has been my home ever since. It has been a lifetime of memories . . . great memories.

Stadiums are just brick and mortar, but the men who played on the field and the fans who cheered in the stands made RFK an unforgettable place to be eight Sundays every fall. There may have been nicer stadiums at Kansas City, Atlanta, Minneapolis and other cities, but how many Super Bowls have those teams won? It's not how nice the stadium looks, but how well you play on the field.

Winning makes for traditions, and RFK has certainly been home to many great games. The authors of this book have chosen 12 memorable games. Remember the Redskins rallying from a 21-0 first-half deficit against the Dallas Cowboys to win 34-31 in 1965? Don't forget the NFL's highest-scoring game ever when the Redskins beat the Giants 72-41 in 1966. How about the 1972 NFC Championship victory over Dallas 26-3? Remember the seat cushions flying from the stands in the 24-7 playoff victory over Atlanta en route to the 1991 championship? Those are games that Redskins fans will always treasure.

What about special plays? Who can forget Ken Houston tackling Walt Garrison at the one-yard line to save a 14-7 victory in 1973? How about Darrell Green defending the pass at the goal line against Minnesota for a 17-10 victory in the 1987 NFC Championship or the time he ran down Tony Dorsett as a rookie when no one thought catching the Cowboys running back from behind was possible? Who could ever forget John Riggins taking a bow at midfield?

You certainly can't win without great players. The Redskins have a long list. Sonny Jurgensen, Russ Grimm, Joe Jacoby, Art Monk, Jeff Bostic, Pat Fischer, Chris Hanburger, Joe Theismann, Doug Williams, Riggins . . . guys who knew what it took to reach the Super Bowls. And don't forget Bobby Mitchell, Charley Taylor, Billy Kilmer, Brian Mitchell, Len Hauss, Mark Moseley, Mark Rypien, Dave Butz and the many other great Redskins who are too numerous to mention.

There have also been some great coaches of the burgundy and gold. Joe Gibbs, George Allen and Vince Lombardi made the Redskins and RFK an unbeatable combination. Gibbs was recently enshrined in the Hall of Fame after 12 wonderful seasons and three Super Bowl titles. Allen took the team to the playoffs five times from 1971-77, including Super Bowl VII. However, I credit Lombardi as the person who started the turnaround. Despite coaching only the 1969 team before his death, Lombardi made the Redskins winners for the first time in 14 years with a 7-5-2 record.

Will we miss RFK Stadium next year when the Redskins leave? Certainly, but it's time to move on. We all want to hang on to tradition, but under today's rules of free agency and the salary cap, playing in RFK is no longer financially possible. But that doesn't mean the players and fans can't start a new tradition. Remember, it's all about the men on the field and fans in the stands. That won't ever change.

Sam Huff played for the Washington Redskins from 1964-67 and 1969, and is a member of the NFL Hall of Fame. He's currently a member of the Redskins radio broadcast team.

ALL-TIME RFK TEAM

OFFENSE

QUARTERBACK .... Sonny Jurgensen

RUNNING BACKS .... John Riggins, Larry Brown

CENTER .... Len Hauss

GUARDS .... Russ Grimm, Mark May

TACKLES .... Joe Jacoby, Jim Lachey

TIGHT END .... Jerry Smith

RECEIVERS .... Art Monk, Charley Taylor

DEFENSE

ENDS .... Charles Mann, Dexter Manley

TACKLES .... Dave Butz, Diron Talbert

LINEBACKERS .... Chris Hanburger, Ken Harvey, Sam Huff

SAFETIES .... Ken Houston, Brig Owens

CORNERBACKS .... Pat Fischer, Darrell Green

SPECIAL TEAMS

KICKER .... Mark Moseley

PUNTER .... Mike Bragg

KICK RETURNER .... Brian Mitchell

COACH .... **Joe Gibbs**

ALL-TIME RFK TEAM

SONNY JURGENSEN LEADS WASHINGTON TO A THRILLING VICTORY OVER DALLAS.

A Sonny Finish

Redskins 34, Cowboys 31

They booed the man they loved more than any other, dumping the blame at his feet. And they chanted for some guy named Shiner. That's what 20 years of futility does to a crowd. Hostilities can run deep. But imagine that. Bench Sonny Jurgensen. Bring in Dick Shiner. Who?

On this day, no one was safe. Not even a beloved passer on the road to the Hall of Fame. But when two of your first four passes are picked off and when the star running back fumbles twice in one half, Washington's fans can turn nasty.

That also happens when the playoffs are again unreachable. For the 20th straight season. In that span, the Redskins finished a combined 89-150-10 and over .500 only three times. That left the fans ready to pounce on anything that went wrong, especially in a season that started with rich expectations.

By the end of this game, however, their tone had changed. And, once again, no one owned the town more than Jurgensen, director of all things heroic.

"All the people who were booing were standing on their feet cheering at the end," recalled linebacker Sam Huff, who had been traded to Washington in 1964.

As for Shiner, he remained pinned to the bench as he did for most of the three years he was in Washington. Since he was a backup, however, that made him popular in the nation's capital, starting a trend that hasn't ended.

Plus, he had played at the University of Maryland, which made him a local favorite. But bench Jurgensen for Shiner? How tough was this crowd? In the fourth game that season, Shiner did start for Jurgensen because in the first three games the offense scored only 24 points. But with Shiner, Washington lost to St. Louis, 37-16. And Jurgensen returned the following week.

"They were putting all the blame on me," said Jurgensen, who went on to have his worst season with the Redskins with 15 touchdowns and 16 interceptions. "We were getting our brains beat out [against St. Louis] and [the coaches] told me to go in and I said, 'What do you think, that I have a 38-point play in my pocket? You made your bed, hey, good luck. Now you're seeing it wasn't me.' "

It's doubtful Shiner, could have rallied the team from a 21-0 deficit. But that's what Jurgensen did against Dallas, throwing two touchdown passes in the game's final

2:16. He finished with 411 yards and three touchdowns passing and another one running.

Sarcastically, Jurgensen told reporters afterwards, "I'm glad the crowd let me stay in. It was decent of them and maybe [coach] Bill McPeak appreciates it, too."

In reality, Jurgensen was used to being booed.

"They did that a lot," Jurgensen said. "But they had every right to do it [that game]. We were a team that struggled. But we had the offensive firepower and we just kept plugging away."

Besides, the booing was much worse in Philadelphia where Jurgensen's career started in 1957. He was a backup to Norm Van Brocklin until 1961. Jurgensen's first season as a starter ended with 32 touchdown passes and a 10-4 record, but the Eagles were in decline and, as usual, the fans blamed the quarterback when the team recorded 3-10-1 and 2-10-2 seasons, respectively, in 1962-63.

It could even be dangerous in Philadelphia after a win.

"We won a game once against the Redskins and [center] Chuck Bednarik told me to put my helmet on

REDSKINS 34, COWBOYS 31					
	1	2	3	4	Total
Cowboys	14	7	3	7	31
Redskins	0	6	7	21	34

FIRST QUARTER
D — Dunn 6 pass from Meredith (Villanueva kick), D 7-0
D — Green 5 run with fumble (Villanueva kick), D 14-0

SECOND QUARTER
D — Gaechter 60 run return of a blocked FG attempt (Villanueva kick), D 21-0
W — Taylor 26 pass from Jurgensen (kick blocked), D 21-6

THIRD QUARTER
D — Villanueva 30 FG, D 24-6
W — Jurgensen 1 run (Jencks kick), D 24-13

FOURTH QUARTER
W — Lewis 2 run (Jencks kick), D 24-20
D — Clarke 53 pass from Meredith (Villanueva kick), D 31-20
W — Mitchell 10 pass from Jurgensen (Jencks kick), D 31-27
W — Coia 5 pass from Jurgensen (Jencks kick), W 34-31

Charley Taylor helps the Redskins rally from a 21-0 deficit.

have thrown 10 touchdown passes."

On April Fool's Day 1964, new Eagles coach Joe Kuharich — who had coached the Redskins from 1954-58 — traded Jurgensen to Washington for quarterback Norm Snead. Jurgensen had just left a meeting with Kuharich, who assured the redhead he wasn't the problem with the Eagles. Then, a couple hours later while sitting in a Philadelphia delicatessen, someone informed Jurgensen he'd been traded to the Redskins. At first, he was shocked. Eventually, he was elated.

going off the field," Jurgensen said. "I said, 'Why?' He said, 'You'll find out.' They threw full beer cans at me. And we had won. I said, 'Wait a minute. What happens when I play poorly?' "

In that case, even your friends boo.

On Nov. 26, 1961, Philadelphia played Dallas and the Franklin Field crowd hooted Jurgensen from the start.

"They booed me coming onto the field," Jurgensen said. "They booed badly. I get in the huddle and the players in the huddle are [jokingly] booing me. I said, 'Hey, come on lighten up. We've got a game to play.' My first pass of the game was intercepted. Boy, it was like everyone was coming on the field. I couldn't believe it. My second pass of the game was intercepted and now they're all coming out. There's a fight breaking out behind the bench. Fans are throwing things. It was just brutal."

By game's end, Jurgensen had thrown five touchdown passes. That helped a little bit.

"I had a friend at the time who said, 'Sonny, I want to tell you something. I'm your friend, but you were bad. I booed too.' I said, 'That's nice, you're a friend and you're booing?' He said, 'I felt like I was out of place by not booing.'

"By the time the third quarter was up, I'd thrown five touchdown passes and there was just a smattering of applause. The rest of the people were embarrassed. They were just sitting there. If I had stayed in, I would

"It was the best thing that ever happened to me," Jurgensen said.

Ditto for the Redskins.

That's why a little booing didn't bother him in his new city. Besides, as he said, it was deserved on this day. Also, Washington entered the year with high expectations after a 6-8 finish in 1964 only to lose its first five games in '65. By the time the Dallas game rolled around, the Redskins had recovered to win four of their last five and were fighting for second place in the Eastern Conference. In that stretch, the offense averaged 23 points and the defense allowed 14.4 points a game.

Dallas entered with a 4-6 record. Though this rivalry escalated under Washington coach George Allen in the 1970s, it was still intense. The Redskins didn't want to be upstaged by a 6-year-old franchise. And Dallas, whose roster included Don Meredith, Dan Reeves, Mel Renfro, Jethro Pugh, Bob Lilly and Bob Hayes, thought it was better than Washington.

The Redskins' Charley Taylor, a Grand Prairie, Tex., native, said, "One thing that made the game big is that [many on the Redskins] were from Texas. For me to go home during the offseason and live, we had to play well against Dallas. If not, it was miserable to live down there. You didn't want to walk the streets at home. If Dallas would beat us, my sister and brother would catch hell all week. All year."

But the D.C. Stadium crowd of 50,205 was silenced early as turnover after turnover left the Redskins in a deep hole. A 21-0 hole.

A Jurgensen fumble, returned 41 yards by Lilly, set up a 6-yard touchdown pass; a Taylor fumble — on third- and-33 from his own 2 — was returned for a touchdown by safety Cornell Green and it was 14-0. Finally, the Redskins recovered a fumble and drove downfield. But, on a 35-yard field goal attempt, disaster struck again. Bob Jencks' kick was blocked by Mike Gaechter, who recovered the ball and sprinted 60 yards for a score.

"It was a bad day for everybody," Taylor said. "We were just fumbling, fumbling. It's not that we were afraid of Dallas [which won the first meeting 27-7]. It's just that things weren't clicking.

"[But] I remember one thing Sonny said. We're down, getting killed and he said, 'We're at home, we can't get beat like this.' Then all of a sudden the plays start happening. We're making first downs, catching the ball. We started fighting our way back. Once we got that momentum going, we started making plays that we weren't making in the first half."

Taylor, the star running back and rookie of the year in 1964, was struggling as much as Jurgensen. Taylor had fumbled twice in the first half, losing one. Jurgensen misfired on his first four passes, two of which were picked off, and he fumbled.

But Taylor and Jurgensen hooked up before half-time to give the Redskins some life. Following a missed 25-yard Dallas field goal attempt by Danny Villanueva, Jurgensen led an 80-yard drive and finished it with a 26-yard touchdown pass to Taylor. Naturally, the extra point was blocked.

If not for the Redskins' defense — helped by Huff, linebacker Chris Hanburger and safety Paul Krause — the score could have been much worse than 21-6 at half-time. The defense came through again in the second half when Taylor fumbled at the Redskins 42 — one of seven fumbles on the day for Washington. Soon it was 24-6. Again, Jurgensen led a long drive, this time a 13-play, 90-yarder that ended with him sneaking over from the 1.

When running back Danny Lewis scored from the 2 early in the fourth quarter, Washington had sliced the lead to 24-20. But the Redskins appeared stopped when Jurgensen was picked off again and Meredith tossed a 53-yard touchdown to receiver Frank Clarke for a 31-20 lead with just under six minutes remaining.

It didn't take the Redskins long to score. Jurgensen passed to receiver Bobby Mitchell for 15; to receiver Angelo Coia for 39 and then to Mitchell for 10 and a touchdown with 3:32 remaining.

The Redskins defense stiffened again, this time following a 56-yard kickoff return to the Washington 41. When Villanueva missed a 45-yarder, the Redskins needed 80 yards in 1:41. No problem.

"You knew Sonny could put points on the board as fast as anyone," Huff said. "With Bobby Mitchell and Charley Taylor, you had three Hall of Famers in that passing game."

How much had Jurgensen's fortune changed since the first quarter? On first-and-10 from the 20, Jurgensen fumbled again. But he recovered and even gained nine yards. Tight end Jerry Smith drew a 19-yard pass interference penalty and followed it with a 22-yard reception to Dallas' 40. Then Mitchell caught a 35-yard pass at the 5 — catching a low pass while nearly bent over — with 1:14 remaining. On first down, Coia sprinted toward the middle, faked a crackback block, then cut back sharply toward the corner where he caught the go-ahead touchdown pass.

But Dallas had 1:04 remaining, enough time to make it too interesting. The Cowboys drove to the Redskins' 34, thanks in large part to a 35-yard pass to Hayes. But the drive stalled and they settled for a 44-yard field-goal attempt with seven seconds to play.

There, a trio of Redskins saved the day. First, Huff and 14-year veteran lineman Fred Williams, needed to clear an opening for 6-foot-3 defensive back Lonnie Sanders. The two would be lined up over the center; Sanders would leap over them.

Huff told Sanders: "We'll open an alley for you, Lon. Go to it."

They did. And he did. Sanders' block capped the best comeback ever by Washington.

It was the biggest win in McPeak's 5-year career. But Washington finished 6-8 and at season's end, the coach was fired after posting a 21-46-3 overall record.

"Bill was a players' coach," Mitchell said. "He understood players. He could handle the old pros, the beer-drinking guys who were like coaches themselves. Bill could fit in with them, let them be the leaders, but still be the coach. He was closer to us than a [Vince] Lombardi or George Allen. The thing that bothered me was that Bill never got credit for how good a coach he was. It's like coaching Northwestern. People say Bill didn't win that many games, but nobody did coaching the Redskins back then."

No one wanted to quibble with McPeak on Nov. 28. Rather, everyone was in the mood to heap praise. Outside the players' entrance, a huge crowd waited for the Redskins to emerge. Everyone basked in the victory. Because the playoffs were always a lost cause, wins like this left the town in a celebrating mood.

"After winning a game like that in those years, the satisfaction was a lot different than it is today," said Mitchell, who needed smelling salts near the end of the game after getting roughed up on a play. "It was like winning a Super Bowl. Today it seems more routine because they can think about the playoffs and all that. Back then, we didn't have a lot to look forward to. Guys hugged each other after a win like that and went through the same emotions you would have today if you won a playoff game."

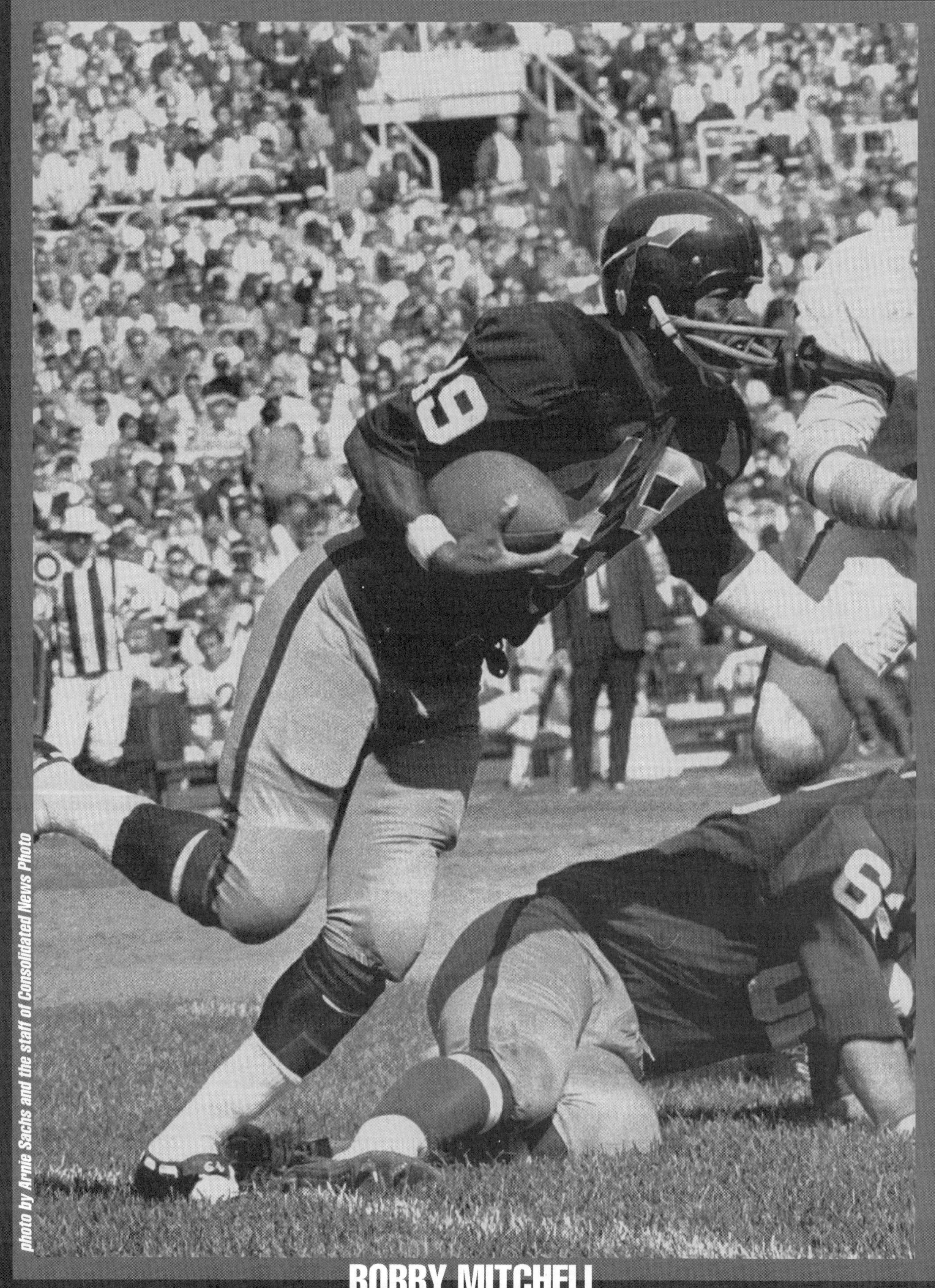

BOBBY MITCHELL

Bobby Mitchell

If D.C. Stadium hadn't been built on government land, Bobby Mitchell might have never become a Redskin.

Washington was in many ways still a Southern city in 1961. Redskins owner George Preston Marshall, who had never employed a black player, had no plans to join the rest of the NFL and change that policy. But Secretary of the Interior Stewart Udall threatened to evict the Redskins from their new stadium if they didn't integrate their team.

Mitchell, a world-record hurdler and a star halfback at Illinois, had averaged more than 800 yards of offense during his first four NFL seasons, but all-Pro runner Jim Brown was always Cleveland's focal point and Mitchell was in some ways a luxury.

The once-powerful Browns, on the verge of losing a fourth straight Eastern Conference crown, coveted Heisman Trophy winner Ernie Davis to team with Brown in an all-Syracuse backfield. Davis had already indicated that he didn't want to be the first black player in Washington. So Marshall traded the first pick in the 1962 draft to Browns owner/coach Paul Brown for Mitchell and LeRoy Jackson. Remarkably, the deal allowed Mitchell to finish 1961 with Cleveland before becoming Washington's first black player.

"I was in the Army at Ft. Meade [Md.] and I would only go back to Cleveland for weekends," Mitchell remembered. "[Defensive end] John Paluck of the Redskins was at Ft. Meade too and he kept telling me something great was going to happen to the Redskins. Jim Brown came up to me with four games or so left and he said he was sorry for what was happening. We went to New York for the last game and Paul Brown wouldn't give me the ball. Guys were yelling at him to give me the ball, but he wouldn't until the fourth quarter. And we lost. Paul was not an emotional guy, but he came up to me after the game and said, 'We're going to miss you.' I didn't know what to say.

"Then [Redskins coach] Bill McPeak called and asked me to come see him. Jim Brown and I used to say whoever was going to be the first black player on the Redskins was going to be a lucky guy. We would ride the bus and see all the black people. I didn't know it was a Southern town."

It didn't take Mitchell, who had grown up in segregated Hot Springs, Ark., long to find out. Free of Brown's shadow and moved to receiver by McPeak, he set club records with a league-leading 72 catches, 1,384 yards and 12 touchdowns in 1962 en route to the first of three straight Pro Bowls. However, that wasn't enough to make some accept him.

"The first two years were very frustrating," Mitchell said. "I wasn't accepted by a lot of the white guys on the team. The fans would yell 'Run, nigger, run.' I was spit on in Duke Zeibert's, [a downtown restaurant.] But I found out quickly that how I handled myself made a world of difference. A lot of things happened to me, but as long as the black kids saw me stay within myself and not lash out, they would stay within themselves and not lash out. It put pressure on me because I wanted to punch someone. If I focused only on my first two or three years here, I would have to be crazy to like anybody in town. As blacks got involved in more things, there weren't as many people on my butt. It never ended. It just got easier."

The games were the easy part. A dazzling runner and gifted receiver, Mitchell ranked second in total yards, catches and touchdowns on kick returns when he retired. He was elected to the Hall of Fame in 1983.

"Bobby could take a pitch to the short side of the field and take that sucker 60, 70 yards," said safety Brig Owens.

"I used to ask Bobby, 'Where do you come up with moves like that?'" raved quarterback Sonny Jurgensen. "Bobby was a tremendous threat to have. Just put one guy on him and Bobby was going to beat him."

The start to Mitchell's Washington career was painful, but 33 years after becoming a Redskin, Mitchell still is one. When ailing hamstrings forced his retirement after 11 seasons, coach/general manager Vince Lombardi convinced him to join the front office. Mitchell, the assistant GM since 1981, will always wonder how he would have filled the top job, but he knows he holds a special place in the history of his club and his city.

"Bobby laid a lot of foundation," Owens said. "It took a special person to come here. Every time they put Bobby in a position to fail, he succeeded, not just in a small way, but in a major way."

Said Mitchell, "I wished I could have lined up just one day and played without any problems. I never did. I went to the stadium with a bag on my shoulder, a trunk on my back. And when you've got to play like that and still make all-Pro . . . I'm proud of that. When I retired, they had a day for me at the stadium and the crowd went crazy. That took away a lot of the hurt. For my family to see the standing ovation, the genuine appreciation . . . I got choked up. To realize we all had come the distance; that we were all one."

Position: Receiver, halfback.

Years: 1962-68.

Stats: 393 catches, 8,162 total yards.

Greatest season: Led NFL with 72 catches for 1,384 yards and 11 TDs in 1962.

Honors: Pro Bowl, 1962-64; Hall of Fame, 1983.

Today: Assistant general manager, Washington Redskins.

SAM HUFF

Sam Huff

Running back John Riggins wondered why Sam Huff was staring at him. Now a Redskins' radio broadcaster, Huff sometimes watched practice. However, he was an old linebacker and usually looked at the defense.

Talking in the parking lot afterwards, Riggins realized Huff was studying him. "You're wondering if you could take me down," Riggins snorted.

Huff was nearing 50, but he was still thinking about tackling Riggins, whom he nicknamed "The Diesel" during the 1982 Super Bowl season. Fifteen years removed from the sport where his fierce play inspired the television show "The Violent World of Sam Huff" and his name became a machine-gun chant of "Huff! Huff! Huff!" at Yankee Stadium, he was still a linebacker at heart. What Huff wouldn't have given to put Riggo on his butt just one time even if the two Hall of Famers had to do it right there on the asphalt.

"I told him I tackled [Cleveland running back] Jim Brown," Huff said, refusing to be intimidated by Riggins, who was at the height of his career.

Huff was one of the greatest linebackers ever. He was voted to the NFL's All-1950s team, made six Pro Bowls, led the New York Giants to the title game in six of eight seasons and graced a 1959 cover of Time magazine. Growing up in a West Virginia coal mining town gave Huff a tireless work ethic and a mean streak that intimidated others on and off the field. You simply didn't mess with Huff. Brown even had trouble getting the better of Huff's crunching hits.

"I was scared to death Brown would have a great day and run all over me," Huff said. "I just locked my jaw and said, 'Brother, you're not going to have it today.' "

Huff played five seasons for the Redskins, including 1969 when he was lured back from a one-year retirement by incoming coach Vince Lombardi. But Huff's best years were history. He made the 1964 Pro Bowl with the Redskins, but that was his peak season. But the Redskins already knew he was nearing the end of his prime. They wanted Huff for two reasons — to room with quarterback Sonny Jurgensen and to teach the perennially losing team how to win.

Huff rooming with Jurgensen was like "The Odd Couple." Huff was asleep by 11 p.m. when Jurgensen was just leaving for his legendary nightlife. Still, they became good friends despite Huff's hatred of quarterbacks and Jurgensen's disdain for linebackers. Indeed, for the last 15 seasons, they have broadcast Redskins games as the popular "Sonny, Sam and Frank [Herzog]" that often becomes a running argument over offense versus defense.

"Sonny loves the passing game and I love the hitting game," Huff said. "We have a lot of respect for each other and what we know about the game."

Huff wasn't enough to make the Redskins winners until his last season at 7-5-2. However, the worst the Redskins fared with Huff was 6-8 compared to 3-11 the year before his arrival.

"It's hard to change a culture," Huff said. "I said to myself, 'Keep your mouth shut, do your job and lead by example.' We had some players, but the culture and front office wasn't there."

Linebacker Chris Hanburger played four seasons with Huff, who taught him to never to let up on opponents.

"When somebody was down, Sam just wanted to bury them," Hanburger said.

You better believe it, Huff said. Otherwise, you might as well not play at all.

CHARLEY TAYLOR SCORES SIX OF WASHINGTON'S RECORD 72 POINTS.

Let the Points Soar

Redskins 72, Giants 41

Otto Graham didn't fancy those 3-0 victories. The Redskins' first-year coach yawned at such affairs. Nope, he'd almost rather spruce up a loss — say 31-30 — than bore with a win. He really didn't have a choice, however. In 1966, his first year in Washington, the Redskins had little defense. And they had a lot of offense.

Some weeks, they had neither. One game, they'd hold a team to 13 points and lose. Another time, they'd score 30 and still lose. Hardly the road a playoff wannabe could afford to travel. But the Redskins didn't need to worry about that, either. Yet another season would pass without a trip to the postseason.

Still, their offense was one of the league's best. They had future Hall of Famers at quarterback (Sonny Jurgensen) and wide receiver (Bobby Mitchell and Charley Taylor). Taylor was switched fulltime from running back to receiver midway through 1966 and, though he says he wasn't comfortable, neither were the defenders covering him.

Stick tight end Jerry Smith, the best at that position in team history, in that group and stopping them was usually too much to ask. By season's end, Taylor, Smith and Mitchell all ranked in the top 10 in catches and in 1967, they would rank first, second and fourth in the league — highest ever by three receivers on the same team. Washington even had one of the game's best centers in Len Hauss. Yes, offense did put fans in the stands as D.C Stadium was sold out for the sixth straight game on Nov. 27, 1966.

That's the excitement Graham wanted. Shortly after he was hired, the ex-Cleveland Browns star quarterback told The Washington Post, "I realize that winning is the most important thing in pro football, but I think you have to put on a show, too. Let's say Charlie Gogolak kicks a field goal and we win, 3-0. That's good. Maybe we will win several close games like that. Fine.

"But I'd rather risk losing some games by say, 35-28, and have the fans up off their seats with excitement."

But who could have predicted the points' explosion against the New York Giants? Or the records that were shattered in this 72-41 victory?

By game's end, the teams had combined to break three NFL records and tie three others. It was the highest scoring game in history. The Redskins set a record for the most points by one team in a regular season game.

The teams combined for a record 16 touchdowns. All three marks still stand. Other records tied that day: most touchdowns, one team (10); most extra points, both teams (14) and most extra points, one team (nine).

Also, the officials lost 16 balls as fans snatched them up after kicks.

"I had never seen so many freak plays," Jurgensen said. "I got tired running on and off the field more than anything else. You weren't out on the field very long."

Redskins safety Brig Owens said, "It was a game that you never thought was going to end. We were just having a lot of fun playing it."

Certainly, the Giants weren't. But neither offense was on the field for long stretches. If the Redskins defense wasn't scoring touchdowns, they were giving them up. And it's not as if New York had a good offense. That season, the Giants finished 11th of 15 teams in scoring and they only won once. Naturally, it was a 13-10 win over the Redskins on Oct. 16.

REDSKINS 72, GIANTS 41

	1	2	3	4	Total
Giants	0	14	14	13	41
Redskins	13	21	14	24	72

FIRST QUARTER
W — Whitfield 5 pass from Jurgensen (kick blocked), W 6-0
W — Whitfield 63 run (C. Gogolak kick), W 13-0

SECOND QUARTER
W — Owens 62 fumble return (C. Gogolak kick), W 20-0
NY — Jacobs 6 run (P. Gogolak kick), W 20-7
W — Whitfield 1 run (C. Gogolak kick), W 27-7
W — Looney 9 run (C. Gogolak kick), W 34-7
NY — Wood 1 run (P. Gogolak kick), W 34-14

THIRD QUARTER
NY — Morrison 41 pass from Wood (P. Gogolak kick), W 34-21
W — Taylor 32 pass from Jurgensen (C. Gogolak kick), W 41-21
NY — Jones 50 pass from Wood (P. Gogolak kick), W 41-28
W — Taylor 74 pass from Jurgensen (C. Gogolak kick), W 48-28

FOURTH QUARTER
W — Harris 52 punt return (C. Gogolak kick), W 55-28
W — Owens 60 pass interception (C. Gogolak kick), W 62-28
NY — Thomas 18 pass from Kennedy (kick failed), W 62-34
NY — Lewis 1 run (P. Gogolak kick), W 62-41
W — Mitchell 45 run (C. Gogolak kick), W 69-41
W — C. Gogolak 29 FG, W 72-41

Six weeks after that low-scoring affair, Washington was ready, even though it had lost three straight games to fall to 5-6.

Middle linebacker Sam Huff was certainly prepared. In 1964, Giants coach Allie Sherman traded Huff to Washington for popular running back Dick James, who set a Redskins record in 1961 with four touchdowns in a game, and defensive lineman Andy Stynchula. Huff, a part of the Giants' 1956 championship team and five others that lost in the title game, was stunned. And angry.

So he was quite pleased when Graham decided 69 points wasn't enough. And with seven seconds remaining, Graham ordered Gogolak onto the field for a 29-yard field goal. Newspaper accounts after the game credited guard Vince Promuto, stung by the memory of a 53-0 loss to the Giants in 1960, with calling a timeout to make sure Gogolak, whose brother Pete was the Giants kicker, had enough time to set up for the attempt.

But Huff and Jurgensen insist the ex-Giant stopped the clock.

"I was on the sidelines saying, 'Why did you call a timeout?' " Jurgensen said. "The word I got was they wanted to let Charlie kick under pressure. I said, 'What kind of pressure is 69-41?' That was all Sam's doing."

Players on the sidelines pleaded for the field goal. Graham obliged.

Later, Graham said he wanted Gogolak to get some work kicking field goals. All he'd done all day is try 10 extra points.

"What's the difference between 69 and 72?" Graham asked afterwards.

Huff said, "I wouldn't have kicked it against any other team. But against the Giants it was beautiful. That's the way I [felt] about [Sherman]."

Two days after the game, though, Graham apologized for the extra three points.

But the difference in those three points was this: They set the regular-season game scoring record, breaking the old mark of 70 set in 1950 by the Los Angeles Rams. Of course, longtime Washingtonians hadn't forgotten the 73-0 debacle against Chicago in the 1940 NFL World Championship. So, against the Giants, the 50,459 in attendance relished another three points.

"Most people would think that was done maliciously," receiver Bobby Mitchell said. "But I honestly believe that old Otto was just caught up in the game. When you've been getting your butt kicked like we had been and then everything's going great, you're enjoying it and you don't want it to ever end. It was a very natural thing to say, 'Kick the field goal.' The Giants were mad of course and they never forgot that. It was very embarrassing for them."

But not for ex-Giants, particularly one named Huff.

"It was a vendetta game for him," Jurgensen said.

The Giants coach pretended to ignore the last act of scoring indecency.

"A coach isn't worth anything if he has to worry more about his own ego than his ballclub," Sherman said. "If they chose to do it, that's OK."

It was a breakout game for the Redskins' offense, which had scored only three points in a loss to Cleveland the week before.

How well did the day go versus New York? Even the defense scored two touchdowns, both by Owens.

The first one followed two scores by running back A.D. Whitfield that made it 13-0. He scored three touchdowns the first four times he touched the ball, including his only two rushing touchdowns of the season. Then it was Owens' turn. He scooped up a fumble caused by linebacker Chris Hanburger and raced 62 yards for the score.

In the third quarter, Owens intercepted a pass — one of three on the day for him — and returned it 60 yards for a touchdown.

"The ball was being turned over so fast and we were scoring so fast, the next thing you know, you're right back on the field," Owens said. "But when you're having that much fun, you don't even think about being tired. It was one of those games you dream about playing, a once-in-a-lifetime game. The ball's flying all over the place and you're right there on top of it."

It's not like the Redskins' offense put up mind-boggling statistics. Besides the score, that is. Jurgensen completed 10-of-16 passes for 145 yards and three touchdowns. Taylor caught six passes for 124 yards, but no other Redskin had more than 12 yards receiving.

Whitfield rushed six times for 74 yards as the Redskins accumulated 342 yards — 47 yards less than the Giants. Washington even punted more than New York — six to four.

And the Giants held the edge in first downs, 25 to 16. But the Redskins picked off five passes, scored on four offensive plays longer than 30 yards and even used a 52-yard punt return for a score by Rickie Harris. That's why their smallest lead after halftime was 13 points. However, they couldn't relax. After the Redskins took a 41-21 third-quarter lead, the Giants scored another touchdown.

"At one point, I asked Sam, 'How many points do we have to get to win this game?' " Jurgensen said.

But they made it 49-28 on Jurgensen's 74-yard pass to Taylor along the right sideline, splitting the Giants' zone coverage. It appeared the safety, running up at Taylor, might pick it off. Looks were deceiving and Taylor scored easily. Earlier in the quarter, he had caught a 32-yard pass.

"And I dropped a sure touchdown pass so it should have been 79 points," Taylor said. "I was 60 yards downfield, no one was there but me and the officials. I heard the [official] running down the sideline and it distracted me and the ball fell. I should have caught that one."

Washington's last touchdown provided a glimpse of Mitchell's past days with Cleveland when he played running back. The Redskins switched him to receiver after they traded for him in 1962.

But in 1966, Graham benched Mitchell because he didn't like his blocking. Mitchell entered the game at flanker to boos in the third quarter — "Maybe I've been here too long," he said after the game — then was moved to running back. On his first run, he gained nine yards.

"I didn't want to go back there," Mitchell said. "But we were short of runners. I hadn't been back there in years. Then the first damn play Sonny calls is an end run for me going to the left. The thing that's so funny about it is he called it and said, 'Break' right away. I said, 'What?' He knew I didn't want to do it. He rushed us to the line. I was still fussing when the ball was snapped."

In the fourth quarter, on his second run, Mitchell had the crowd cheering him again. He ripped through a hole on the right side and dashed 45 yards for a touchdown.

"That old instinct took over," Mitchell said. "A guy came up to make the tackle and I just stopped, cut and 'Pop' I was gone. I was in the end zone so quick.

"I don't know why I did it. I came back to the sidelines just as mad. [Baltimore's] Lenny Moore had gone back to running back [from receiver] and messed up his knee. Why would I want to go back to running back? Otto knew I could run from my being in Cleveland and he had been threatening to put me back there. He would say, 'I've got my best running back playing receiver.' There was some truth to that, but at the same time, I would be saying, 'Hey, man. I'm not that young anymore.' When you make a run like that, everyone on the team says, 'We've got receivers . . .' Once you get that ball, it's automatic."

Everything was automatic that day and that year on offense. Jurgensen, who had reported to camp at a svelte 192 pounds, finished the season with 3,209 passing yards and 28 touchdowns; Taylor led the NFL with 72 catches for 1,119 yards and 12 touchdowns while Mitchell finished with 58 catches for 905 yards and nine scores. Right behind him was Smith with 54 receptions for 686 yards and six touchdowns. That season, the Red-skins scored more than 30 points five times and allowed more than 30 six times.

But nothing they did that season matched what the team accomplished against the Giants.

"It was a total game," Taylor said. "The day the sky rained footballs. It was like, 'Whoa, not another one. Eighty yards, 60 yards. What's happening here?' But they scored 41 points. So they did everything right, too."

Charlie Gogolak sets a record and angers the Giants.

CHARLEY TAYLOR

Charley Taylor

In the huddle, Charley Taylor would hear the play call, pause for a moment to digest the information and then zip to his position. And he'd still run the wrong pattern. Once the next Jim Brown at running back, Taylor felt more like Charlie Brown at his new position.

Taylor didn't lose his desire for football. But he did lose 15 pounds after coach Otto Graham switched him to receiver.

"Because I was worried about it," recalled Taylor, whose first start at receiver came on Oct. 23, 1966, against St. Louis at D.C. Stadium. "Part of that worry was on Sunday afternoons when I made mistakes. Sonny [Jurgensen] would call a play and I'd go, 'Yeah, that's a 15-yard in. You've got to do this, got to do that.' Actually, it would be a 15-yard out. I was like, 'God, how many mistakes can I make.' I'd watch film and count and think, 'This play was called and I screwed it up good.' I was afraid out there every weekend."

So were defensive backs as Taylor had five games with more than 100 reception yards in 1966. Still, he said it took him two years to get comfortable at receiver, though teammate Bobby Mitchell, who made a similar move in 1962, eased the transition. So did quarterback Jurgensen. When Taylor retired in 1977, he was the NFL's all-time leading receiver, a record he broke at RFK against Philadelphia in the fourth quarter of the 1975 season finale, catching an 11-yard pass from Joe Theismann.

"That catch didn't stand out," Taylor said. "I was thinking about the next 40 or 50 I would get. It was great, but I thought, 'Let's step on this thing.' But I got hurt in training camp [shoulder] and didn't play. I broke the record and no one saw me again."

Had injuries not sidelined him for eight games in 1971, all of 1976 and seven more in 1977, Taylor might have had another 100 catches.

And if he'd had his original wish, he would have played with Dallas. When the Redskins won a coin flip with the Cowboys and drafted the Grand Prairie, Tex. native in the first round in 1963, he cried, not wanting to leave the state. His sentiment soon changed.

In his first two seasons as a running back, Taylor was exceptional, amassing 2,559 yards and 16 touchdowns rushing and receiving. He set a record for running backs with 53 receptions as a rookie.

"But Charley was an undisciplined runner," Jurgensen said. "He'd run a sweep, two guards would pull to lead the play and he would pass them. He wouldn't wait. That's why it wasn't working.

"As a receiver, you got him the ball so he could make people miss, run over them or whatever. He was a great athlete. At times, you forced the ball to him because you figured he had a better chance to catch it than the defenders."

One key, aside from precise patterns: no one knew how fast Taylor was. Nearly 20 years after his career ended, Taylor still keeps 'em guessing. One minute, he says he ran the 40-yard dash in 4.8 seconds. About 20 minutes later, he changes that to a 4.5.

"He was as fast as he needed to be," said Redskins safety Ken Houston.

"Evidently there's truth to that because people never caught me," Taylor said. "I just did what I had to get by people. I had great acceleration. If I had to accelerate to a 4.2, I could."

He did it all with a smile. Defensive backs read the smiles, worn even while running patterns, as arrogance.

"That was my personality," said Taylor, who became the Redskins first black assistant coach in 1981, and through 1993. "Rather than upset someone, why not smile at them? It's hard to get ticked off at a guy smiling at you."

But it's easy to get irked at a physical receiver. Taylor, whom teammates said had a mean streak, prided himself in being one of the best blocking receivers in the league. Crackback blocks, where he would blindside the defender, became a specialty. When former teammates discuss Taylor, his blocking is quickly mentioned.

"You had to hit him as hard as you could," said Houston, who played against Taylor once while with the Oilers and later became his fishing buddy. "And he had your head on a swivel, too."

Taylor was an all-round receiver and his career ended with a complete change. He had wanted to become the next Jim Brown at running back. Instead, he became the first Charley Taylor at receiver.

As A Redskin

Position: Wide receiver, running back.

Years: 1964-77.

Stats: 649 receptions for 9,140 yards and club-record 79 touchdowns.

Greatest season: Led NFL with 72 receptions for 1,119 yards and league-best 12 touchdowns in 1967.

Honors: Pro Bowl, 1964-67, 72-75; Hall of Fame, 1984.

Today: Self-employed in construction in Reston, Va.

SONNY JURGENSEN

Sonny Jurgensen

His passing they admired, his physique they adored. Sonny Jurgensen was one of them, the fans thought. At least until the ball was snapped. Then there was no one like him. Forget the round middle and check out those tight spirals. He flipped passes behind his back. He curved others around linebackers.

Conditioning? Why bother. His job was to throw the football. And few have ever done it better.

Fortunately, Jurgensen also passed on a doctor's advice in May of 1968 after undergoing surgery (one of 15 operations) to remove calcium deposits in his right elbow. Afterwards, the doctor delivered bad news.

"He said, 'You should find something else to do,' " Jurgensen remembered. "I said, 'Have you told anyone about this?' He said no. I said, 'Well, don't! That's my profession. I'll compensate as much as I can.' "

Jurgensen returned for the final preseason game. In the season opener, he tossed four touchdown passes and 276 yards in a 38-28 win over Chicago.

"When it comes down to pure passers, there's no question Sonny Jurgensen was [the best]," said Dallas Hall of Fame defensive back Mel Renfro.

Since 1964, Christian Adolph (Sonny) Jurgensen III has meant football in Washington. That's the year he arrived in a trade from Philadelphia for quarterback Norm Snead and defensive back Claude Crabb. In 1982, he joined the Redskins radio team with Sam Huff and Frank Herzog.

These days, there's still no one more popular than the cigar-chomping redhead, always patient and gracious despite being a lightning rod for fans' attention. Jurgensen understood his appeal while playing.

"The [fans would] say, 'Look at him, if he can do it . . . I can sit here, have my six-pack and go out and do something.' [But] I just had a bad tailor. My uniform was cut badly," joked Jurgensen.

The 6-foot, 203-pound Jurgensen worked at his craft in the offseason and he studied the game hard. By the time Jurgensen retired, he had captured three passing titles and owned pro football's third-highest quarterback rating (82.8). He still owns, or shares, six Redskins records including most completions in a game (32); highest career completion percentage (58.0); longest pass completion (99 yards); highest career rating (85.0); most touchdown passes in a season (31) and most consecutive games with a touchdown pass (23).

Everyone called him a pure passer because of his fluid motion. He could throw from all angles and even from behind his back. Jurgensen did that once at Duke and completed the pass for 37 yards, which nearly got him benched. His next, and last, one came in 1961 with Philadelphia in the College All-Star game for a short completion. He then limited those passes to practice. But he still did amazing things.

"Sonny's the only quarterback I've seen that could throw a slider," said Hall of Fame receiver Charley Taylor. "The ball would actually go right around the guy. I don't think it was on purpose. It was natural."

Cornerback Pat Fischer said, "He had a passing arc. And anywhere in that arc, that damn ball might be released. He pulled that trigger anytime."

Jurgensen's favorite season was 1969, the only year Vince Lombardi coached in Washington. In their first meeting, the former Green Bay coach ignored Jurgensen's weight, unlike his previous five head coaches.

But Jurgensen, knowing of Lombardi's brutal practices, reported to camp in the best shape of his career. That season, he led the NFL in passing, completing 62 percent of his passes for 22 touchdowns and helping the team to its first winning season (7-5-2) since 1955. Lombardi called Jurgensen, "the best I've ever seen."

Jurgensen returned those sentiments.

"I loved talking football with [Lombardi]," Jurgensen said. "He simplified the game and made it fun. It was simply the best passing offense I had ever played with."

Too bad he never played with a talented team in his prime.

"Had Sonny [played] with a defense, he would have won more championships than anybody," said strong safety Richie Petitbon, who also played against Jurgensen for the Bears and Rams. "Man, if he had been with Green Bay [in the 1960s], they would have ruined football."

As A Redskin

Position: Quarterback.

Years: 1964-74.

Stats: 1,831 completions in 3,155 attempts for 22,585 yards, 179 touchdowns and 116 interceptions; 85.0 career rating best in franchise history.

Greatest season: Led the league in touchdowns (31), passing yards (3,747), completions (288) and attempts (508) and was second in completion percentage (56.7) in 1967.

Honors: Pro Bowl, 1964, 66, 67, 69; Hall of Fame, 1983.

Today: Redskins radio broadcaster for WJFK, Redskins analyst on WRC-TV, Washington, D.C.

COACH GEORGE ALLEN

George Allen

The stories are true. All of them. Those who knew the late George Allen can rattle off half a dozen in no time. They talk about his love of milk and spending other people's money. Especially the Redskins'. They mention his rah-rah tactics; breakfast habits (oatmeal, raisin bread and grapefruit every day); offseason dinner conversations (football only, please); constant phone calls, drawn-out practices and trades. And everything else that defined the man.

But the biggest story involved winning. And George Herbert Allen, who arrived in Washington in 1971, did that quite often.

From 1946-1970, the Redskins posted four winning seasons and captured no division titles. In Allen's seven years, they always had a winning season, made the playoffs five times, won three division titles and reached the Super Bowl once. At RFK, Allen was 40-10-1, including 2-0 in the playoffs.

"George turned this city around completely and unified it," said Redskins general manager Charley Casserly, who was hired by Allen in 1977 as an unpaid intern. "I think the great enthusiasm that we have in Washington now is that the '70s really got people fired up about the Redskins."

After beating Dallas for the 1972 NFC Championship, Allen said, "Winning in Washington means more than in other places. The fans here have had enough losers. Now they have a winner."

And in a town that loved making deals, no one did it better than Allen. When he was hired, Allen quickly worked the phone lines. Within three weeks of being hired, he pulled the trigger with the team he had just left after five seasons, the Los Angeles Rams: Seven draft choices, plus linebacker Marlin McKeever for linebackers Maxie Baughan, Jack Pardee and Myron Pottios, defensive tackle Diron Talbert, guard John Wilbur and special teams ace Jeff Jordan. And a fifth-round pick. Eventually, Allen acquired 10 former Rams. Soon, people jokingly called the team the Ramskins.

But Allen wasn't done. He made 19 trades involving 33 players before his first training camp.

"If they want another draft choice, give it to them," Allen once said. "What do you care as long as you get the player you want. The future is now."

The last sentence became Allen's motto. During his tenure, the Redskins traded every first-round pick. But he didn't stop with just the first choice. Only once in his seven years did he not trade each of his first four selections. That came in his first season when the team picked receiver Cotton Speyrer in the second round. Before camp opened, Speyrer was shipped to Baltimore for receiver Roy Jefferson.

Allen made more than 80 trades in Washington. In 1973, he even traded the same pick twice. The Redskins were fined and the anti-establishment Allen was lectured by commissioner Pete Rozelle.

Allen's philosophy was to stack the lineup with veterans while grooming younger players. It's no wonder his teams were called "The Over the Hill Gang." But Allen was loyal to players who had helped him win. And he liked adding players whom other teams had abandoned, such as the five players who had previously been union representatives.

"George saw those guys as leaders," said safety Brig Owens. "I remember going to a [players-owners] negotiating meeting one time . . . and one of the owners said George Allen was the worst thing to happen to football. That was probably because he paid his players well and took players nobody wanted."

That's why most of his players loved Allen. What they didn't like was his three-hour practices. But Allen believed in repetition. If a player messed up in a drill — and Owens said Allen saw everything — Allen would start it over. On real bad days, he'd make them go back to calisthenics.

Sloppy huddle breaks also irked Allen.

"We'd practice breaking the huddle for a few minutes," Talbert said. "It seemed like high school stuff, but it makes you do things better. We won games when we were outmanned."

Speaking of high school, Allen believed in creating an atmosphere better suited for teenagers. That can be difficult to sell to a bunch of older players, especially those unfamiliar with Allen. Like center Len Hauss.

A Redskin since 1964, Hauss was one of the best

George Allen congratulates Billy Kilmer, his favorite quarterback.

centers in football, having made the Pro Bowl from 1967-70.

At first, he frowned at Allen's antics. After the Redskins beat St. Louis in their 1971 season opener, Allen gathered his team in the middle of the locker room.

"Let's have three cheers for the Redskins!" he shouted.

Hauss was amazed.

"[Offensive tackle] Walt Rock and I were at our lockers and sat there and looked at each other and our thought is, 'Is this ridiculous or what?' " Hauss recalled. "The next week, we did it again. Walt and I are saying, these are grown men."

But it was hard to defeat Allen's enthusiasm.

"By the fourth week, we were right in the middle of it and getting caught up in it," said Hauss, who earned two more Pro Bowl berths with Allen.

Allen captured the city as well and would often get standing ovations at Duke Zeibert's [restaurant] after victories. Washington's most important resident, President Richard Nixon, suggested plays that his friend, the coach, once used.

Defense was Allen's forte, however. He was an innovator — nickel backs and audibles were his creations in the 1960s as a defensive assistant in Chicago. Both are standard these days. Richie Petitbon, one of the

NFL's best defensive coordinators from 1981-92 who played for Allen in Chicago, Los Angeles and Washington, said he was, "the best defensive coach I have ever seen."

As for offense? Well, Allen ranked it behind even the special teams.

"He didn't care if we scored points," offensive tackle George Starke said. "As long as we didn't give any away."

That caused problems. Quarterback Sonny Jurgensen clashed with Allen for the four years they were together, partly because of the way Allen alternated between Jurgensen and Billy Kilmer.

Conflicts also stemmed from Allen's offensive philosophy. He liked conservative plays; Jurgensen loved to throw. In a 1973 game against San Francisco, Kilmer got hurt and Jurgensen entered on third down at the 18. Allen ordered a draw play, setting up a field goal.

"My thinking is, '[Screw] the draw play,'" Jurgensen remembered. "So I audibled and threw a touchdown. George asked me, 'Why didn't you run the draw play?' I said, 'Well, I came to the line of scrimmage and they were hollering, 'Look out for the draw!' He wouldn't put me back in the game.

"George would always say, 'You're not going along with the system.' That was part of my conflict with him. I wouldn't go along with the system."

But nothing revved Allen more than Dallas week. The Cowboys were one of the best teams in football, having won the year before Super Bowl VI after having lost the title game. From 1966-1970, Dallas compiled a 63-19-2 record and was 8-2 versus Washington. But under Allen, the Redskins finished 7-8 against the Cowboys. Allen would make up stories about Dallas just to rile his players.

And he would often share a fervent wish: Both teams would gather at the 50, Allen and Dallas coach Tom Landry would step forward and duke it out. The last one standing would be the winner.

"We had to have every edge possible," Talbert said. "George would get you rolling during the week. Sometimes he'd get you too high."

Trainer Bubba Tyer, who joined the team in 1971, said, "It was a passion. [The rivalry] was brought on by George Allen and his passion for beating Tom Landry."

Football mattered most to Allen, who was the first to conduct offseason minicamps. Tyer remembers annual offseason dinners for the team doctors, trainers and their wives at expensive restaurants where Allen spent the evenings drawing plays on napkins. Allen's wife Etty once joked that her husband liked ice cream because it didn't take any time to eat and "chewing would take his mind away from football." Those dinners, by the way, were always billed to the Redskins. That's one of the many ways Allen exceeded the "un-limited budget" bestowed on him by owner Edward Bennett Williams.

Another was by looking out for his players. Allen thought they deserved a first-rate facility, rather than the high-school like practice site they had next to RFK, and told Williams so. By June of 1971, construction of Redskin Park in Herndon, Va., had begun.

But Allen wanted to win more than anything else.

Two days after a 24-23 loss to lowly New England in 1972, Brundige recalls Allen shouting, "I would have cut my arm off if it would have made us win that game. No one should get paid. How can you eat? I wish we could play tomorrow. My God! This is losing!"

Allen also once said, "Losing the Super Bowl is worse than death. You have to get up the next morning."

So Allen worked countless hours to give his team the best chance to win.

"We were in the playoffs once over the holidays," Hanburger recalled. "And George was always trying to get extra film from teams to find out about who we were playing. We were practicing on Christmas Day, and he would say 'Can you believe I called so-and-so today and they didn't answer their phone?' "

Allen's family wasn't immune from his fire.

"One time [Allen's teenage son] Bruce was on the sidelines giving the officials a bunch of crap," Owens said. "The referee finally told George he would give us a 15-yard penalty if we didn't get him off the sideline. He asked George, 'Do you know who he is?' George said, 'I don't know. He's not part of our organization. You can't penalize us.' George denied his own son. We were all laughing."

Eventually, the Redskins became exasperated with Allen's autocratic ways and propensity for running up expenses. He left Washington after the 1977 season — both sides decided to explore other options after an apparent contract extension fell through — and returned to Los Angeles, site of his only other head coaching job in the NFL. But Allen became locked in a power struggle and was fired before the season started.

His NFL days were over despite never having had a losing season. Owners simply didn't want to deal with Allen.

But Allen coached in the renegade USFL and later in college. Allen continued to win, but it cost him his life. He died Dec. 31, 1990, after a bout with pneumonia. It was brought on earlier that year when he coached Long Beach State to its first winning season. After the last game, the players doused him with water.

Maybe he didn't win a Super Bowl, but Allen set standards that made such victories all that could be accepted in Washington.

"His record is unbelievable," Casserly said. "He should be in the Hall of Fame. This franchise owes George Allen a lot and the city owes George Allen a lot."

CHARLEY TAYLOR WHIPS MARK WASHINGTON TO CLINCH THE NFC TITLE.

Who's Over the Hill?

Redskins 26, Cowboys 3

In 1972, Washington was not the thriving metropolis it is today. Just four years removed from fiery riots scorching 14th Street, Washington was known as the home of the federal government and little else.

There weren't many fine ethnic restaurants or cultural diversions. The city's baseball team, the Senators, had left for Texas the year before. There was no pro basketball or hockey. University of Maryland basketball was the only college sport with any following.

But Washington did have the Redskins. And in 1972 that was enough. Coach/general manager George Allen had brought his "The Future Is Now" philosophy to Washington in 1971 and the Redskins proved it by finishing 9-4-1 and making the playoffs for the first time since 1945 thanks to Allen's trades for such veterans as quarterback Billy Kilmer, defensive tackle Diron Talbert and linebacker Jack Pardee.

Burgundy and gold became the city's colors of choice and "Hail To The Redskins" its favorite song. A local hospital even printed up bumper stickers which read, "I've Got Redskins Fever." The only Redskins matter Washingtonians disagreed about was whether 1971 starter Kilmer or longtime hero Sonny Jurgensen should be the quarterback in 1972.

"The people were crazy," Talbert said. "You would go around the Beltway and someone would be leaning out the window with a piece of paper wanting an autograph and you're going 60-70 miles per hour. Those people really are the greatest football fans in the country."

Allen, a defensive-minded coach who never trusted the pass-happy Jurgensen, chose Kilmer. But it was all-Pro halfback Larry Brown, the defense and the special teams — featuring kick-blocking specialist Bill Malinchak — which led Washington to victories in its first two games. And after poor tackling and bad officiating produced a one-point upset loss in New England, Jurgensen was back at the helm. The Redskins won three straight, including a wondrous comeback against archrival Dallas at RFK Stadium, but on Oct. 29, Jurgensen's Achilles' tendon snapped at Yankee Stadium. The job belonged to Kilmer again.

The quarterback switch didn't change anything. Washington's winning streak reached nine, the club's longest in 30 years, before Allen rested NFL rushing leader Brown for the final two games with the NFC East title clinched. The Redskins lost both games, including a 34-24 defeat at Dallas, but they had sent the Cowboys a message after trailing 28-3 at halftime at the newly-opened Texas Stadium. And who knows? If Washington had managed to win that New England cliffhanger, Allen may have kept Brown in the lineup and the Redskins might have matched AFC king Miami's record perfect 14-0 season.

"It was like you had something to prove each week, like 'We're not over the hill, we can still kick butt,' " Talbert said. "We made fewer mistakes because of our experience."

Green Bay had experienced Allen's five-man defensive front a month before, but the lesson didn't help as Washington throttled Packers runners John Brockington and MacArthur Lane in a 16-3 playoff victory at RFK. The Redskins' first postseason triumph since 1943 set up an NFC Championship Game showdown with the Cowboys, who had rallied past the 49ers behind quarterback Roger Staubach, back from a shoulder injury.

Dallas coach Tom Landry confirmed that Staubach, who had bedeviled Washington in 1971 at RFK, would start in place of Craig Morton, who had guided the de

<table>
<tr><td colspan="6" align="center">REDSKINS 26, COWBOYS 3</td></tr>
<tr><td></td><td>1</td><td>2</td><td>3</td><td>4</td><td>Total</td></tr>
<tr><td>Cowboys</td><td>0</td><td>3</td><td>0</td><td>0</td><td>3</td></tr>
<tr><td>Redskins</td><td>0</td><td>10</td><td>0</td><td>16</td><td>26</td></tr>
</table>

SECOND QUARTER
W - Knight FG 18, W 3-0
W - Taylor 15 pass from Kilmer (Knight kick), W 10-0
D - Fritsch FG 33, W 10-3

FOURTH QUARTER
W - Taylor 45 pass from Kilmer (Knight kick), W 17-3
W - Knight FG 39, W 20-3
W - Knight FG 46, W 23-3
W - Knight FG 45, W 26-3

fending Super Bowl champions all year. The Cowboys' fearsome lineup also featured halfback Calvin Hill, defensive tackle Bob Lilly, middle linebacker Lee Roy Jordan and cornerback Mel Renfro. Stars as bright as the ones on their silver and blue helmets.

"As usual, George said this was the biggest game of our lives, but this time it was," Owens said. "George said, 'If you just play consistent and be real physical, there's no way they can beat us in RFK. This is our home. We've got our fans. All the electricity and chemistry is on our side. If it takes me to go out in the middle of the field and fight Tom Landry, I'll take him on and whip him too.'"

But as they prepared for the Cowboys, 11 Redskins, including five starters, were riddled with the flu. By Sunday, all were ready to go. Perhaps the visit to Redskin Park by Mayor Walter Washington that week had helped. The mayor reminded the players how important they were to an area often divided by race and by geography: D.C., Maryland and Virginia.

"The mayor said, 'You're the glue that's holding this city together,'" recalled defensive tackle Bill Brundige. "'It doesn't matter if you're black, white, rich or poor, you're a Redskin fan. By winning, you have given every citizen in this city something special to have in common and pull together and root for you guys.'"

On New Year's Eve at RFK, the fans pulled together and rooted for their Redskins as never before. The roar began before the Cowboys were introduced. Allen let it reach fever pitch for almost five minutes before sending captain Charley Taylor onto the field.

The coach's motto was, "40 men together can't lose," but on this afternoon, it was more like 40 plus 53,129.

"The crowd was stamping its feet, banging on the walls," Brundige remembered. "It was so loud. You almost felt like you were standing in the surf and instead of waves of water crashing on us, it was waves of sound. It was an awesome experience."

The only early scoring threat ended when Brown fumbled on the Dallas 30 after catching what looked like a first-down pass from Kilmer. But late in the quarter, Brown and fullback Charley Harraway began breaking good runs and after a nine-minute drive died at the Dallas 11, Curt Knight kicked an 18-yard field goal.

When Washington got the ball back, Kilmer decided to test Charlie Waters, a young safety whom Landry had moved to cornerback in favor of the aging Herb Adderly.

"They were giving me strongside coverage [on Roy Jefferson] and leaving Charley Taylor one-on-one," Kilmer said after the game. "We wanted to pick on the weakest man. It's nothing against Waters so much as we didn't want to go against Renfro. He can make the big play."

This time the big play was made by Kilmer and Taylor. The coverage was good, but the pass was better. It went for 51 yards. Three plays later, Kilmer found Taylor on a 15-yard slant for the touchdown.

Washington led 10-0 with just 5:33 left in the half. Dallas still didn't have a first down. But ex-Cowboy Talbert roughed Staubach on the next play and that seemed to energize the visitors. Thanks to a 29-yard run by Staubach, Dallas drove for a 35-yard field goal by Toni Fritsch. Passes to Ron Sellers and Lance Alworth — the future Hall of Famer who had become suddenly notorious in Washington for an alleged crackback block on Pardee three weeks before — set up another field-goal attempt on the half's final play. However, this one was wide left from 23 yards. It was Fritsch's first miss in 15 tries from inside the 30. The Cowboys wouldn't come that close again.

The third quarter was much like the first as the defenses dominated. The Redskins got lucky when Kilmer's fumble bounced by Waters, Jordan and safety Cornell Green before tight end Jerry Smith recovered at the Washington 18. Perhaps just as important, Waters broke his arm trying to return Mike Bragg's subsequent punt.

Late in the quarter after cornerback Mike Bass had deftly broken up Staubach's bomb for Bob Hayes, the Redskins began a long march on the backs of Brown and Harraway. The lights were on now and Kilmer decided to turn the spotlight on the little-used Mark Washington, whom Landry had put in Waters' place instead of Adderly.

After two short completions to Taylor, Kilmer decided to go long from the Dallas 45. The supposedly rag-armed quarterback heaved the ball as far as he could as Taylor raced under it. Washington dived at Taylor's heels but came up empty as the receiver scored the touchdown which broke the game open. The Redskins led 17-3 just two plays into the final quarter. Taylor raised his hands skyward. Kilmer punched the air in joy and the stadium shook as if in the midst of an earthquake.

"I just told Charley to run as far as he could," Kilmer said. "I thought I had overthrown him. I don't know how he got to it. It was an electrifying moment. It put the game out of reach."

Five plays later, safety Rosey Taylor forced a fumble by Hill at the Dallas 38 and Knight followed soon there

Larry Brown sets off on another run against the hated Cowboys.

after with a 39-yard field goal. Brundige and end Verlon Biggs teamed up to sack Staubach, setting up a 46-yarder by Knight. Bob Brunet leveled Cliff Harris on the ensuing kickoff, sending the crowd into pure ecstasy.

"The stands were rocking," Brundige marveled. "You could literally feel the sound cascading in your body. It was so incredible. Pardee was calling signals in the huddle and I was about a foot and a half from him and he was yelling as loud as he could and I couldn't hear a thing he said. When the Cowboys trotted to the line, you could see their heads turning left and right and you could see going through their minds, 'What in the hell am I doing here?' "

Just trying to get out alive on what was so clearly Washington's day.

Five plays after Staubach's fourth-down pass was broken up by Hanburger, Knight booted a 43-yard field goal to close out the scoring. Charley Taylor and center Len Hauss, the senior Redskins after nine seasons, stared into each other's eyes as if to say, "We finally did it."

Redskins 26, Cowboys 3. Washington was Super Bowl-bound.

The fans swarmed the field and the players, some of whom gave Allen a victory ride in the city's most joyous celebration since V-J Day.

"A lot of people wrote us off as too old, too slow and too heavy," Allen said in the locker room. "Nobody wanted [us]. This is a closer-knit team than any team I've had. They work together, they play together and they love each other. They're like brothers."

That togetherness and talent fell a touchdown short against Miami in the Super Bowl and the Redskins would not win another playoff game under Allen despite five more winning seasons in a row, but that New Year's Eve, George Allen was bigger than Guy Lombardo.

BILLY KILMER

Billy Kilmer

The first trade coach George Allen made after coming to the Washington in 1971 was for quarterback Billy Kilmer. However, Kilmer wasn't too thrilled about coming to the Redskins. After all, they already had Sonny Jurgensen.

Kilmer, 31, thought his career might be over. He had already escaped retirement once after missing the 1963 season when an auto accident nearly caused his foot to be amputated. That injury forced Kilmer to convert from a running quarterback to a passer after rushing for nearly 1,000 yards during his first two seasons. Kilmer had found new life when taken by New Orleans in the 1967 expansion draft and started four years. But now Allen wanted him to back up Jurgensen, who was still going strong.

"I asked George to trade me because I only had a few years left to play and I wanted to be the starting quarterback," Kilmer said.

Instead, Kilmer and Jurgensen became legendary friends and Kilmer played eight years for the Redskins and led them to Super Bowl VII.

"Sonny and I hit it off right away," Kilmer said. "Because we both were in our 30s and had never won at all, we decided to go out winners. We understood we had a good chance to be on a winning team so instead of being petty about things, we decided to help each other. We knew there wasn't one healthy body between us and neither of us could play the whole season."

Kilmer would lead the Redskins in passing for seven years before Joe Theismann replaced him in 1978. But Jurgensen often came off the bench or started, and the two always seemed linked.

"I got my shot to play, and played well," Kilmer said. "George and Sonny had a rivalry so maybe that's why I played more than I should."

The rivalry extended into the stands as fans fiercely chose sides with "I Love Billy" and "I Love Sonny" bumper stickers separating the political town more than Democrats and Republicans.

"George tried to create a rivalry at every position," Kilmer said. "I wasn't surprised that fans took sides. Sonny is the guy, and he always will be. Sometimes I didn't like it, but I accepted it."

Nicknamed "Whiskey" for his legendary partying as part of the Over The Hill Gang and "Furnace Face" for his reddish complexion, Kilmer was beloved by teammates for his toughness. In 1976 against the New York Giants, Kilmer couldn't even see late in the game after a hit by defensive end Jack Gregory that caused blood from his nose to seep into his eyes. After missing one play, Kilmer hit receiver Roy Jefferson on fourth-and-15 for the touchdown to win 19-17. Kilmer's nose would later require six stitches.

"I looked like a car had hit me," he said. "I had told [trainer] Bubba [Tyer] to just get the bleeding stopped. You just played with injuries."

Cornerback Pat Fischer, known as one of the NFL's hardest hitters, said Kilmer was one of the toughest players ever.

"Billy was hurt, but he'd still play and fight you to the end," Fischer said. "He was the type of guy if you needed to go down an alley with somebody, you'd take him with you."

Said safety Ken Houston: "Billy was gutty. He'd have a hard time walking in a lot of instances."

Kilmer's greatest moment came in the 1972 NFC Championship Game against Dallas. The Redskins pounded their rivals 26-3 to advance to the Super Bowl with Kilmer completing 14-of-18 passes for 194 yards and two touchdowns. His 45-yard touchdown pass to Charley Taylor remains Kilmer's favorite RFK memory.

"That put it out of reach," Kilmer said. "There was just an explosion of screams."

And plenty of good times. Not bad for someone who didn't want to come to Washington.

As A Redskin

Position: Quarterback.

Years: 1971-78.

Stats: Completed 953 of 1,791 passes for 12,352 yards and 103 touchdowns.

Greatest season: Completed 178 of 346 passes for 2,440 yards and 23 touchdowns in 1975.

Honors: Pro Bowl, 1972.

Today: Retired, Fort Lauderdale, Fla.

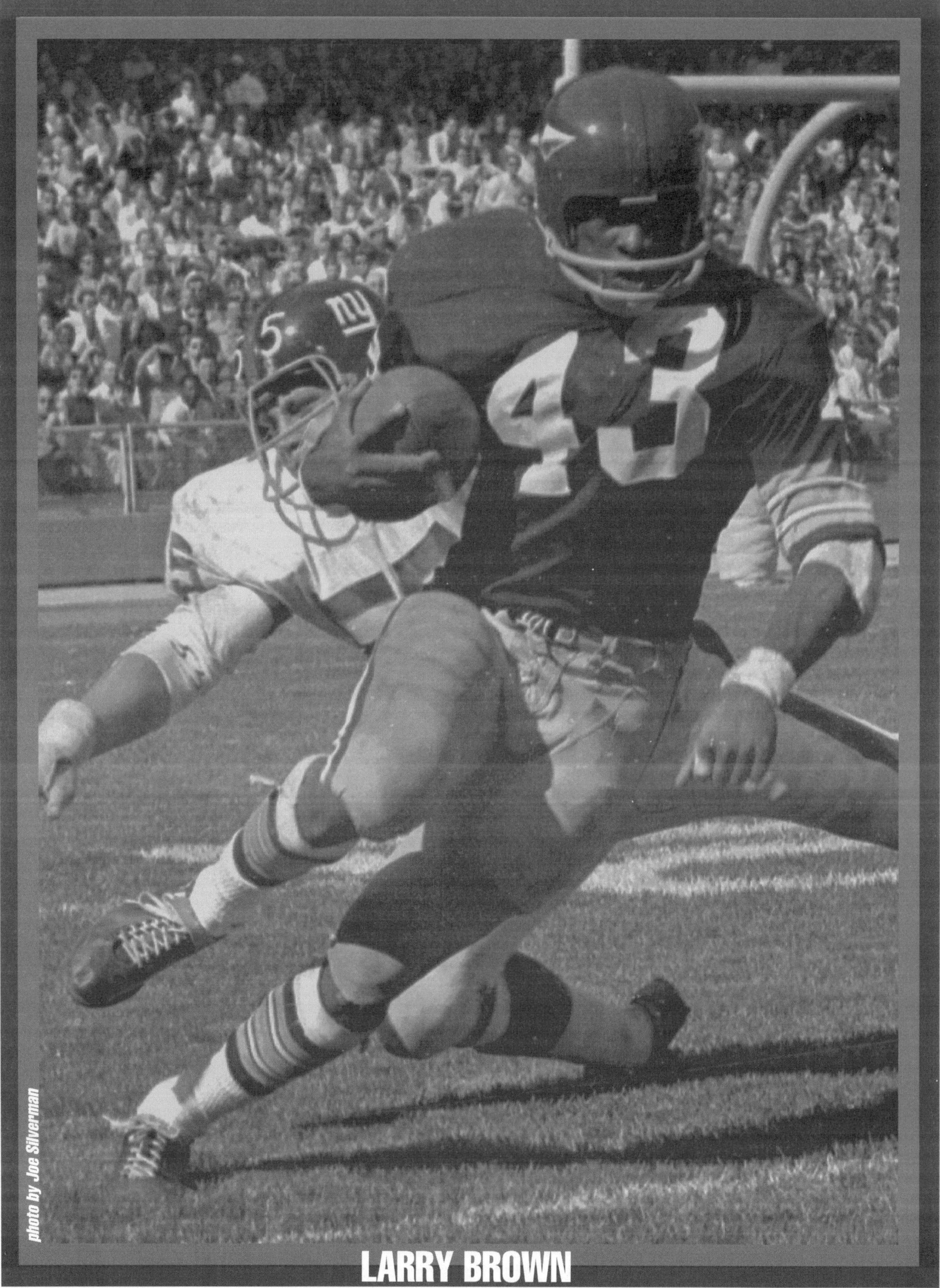

LARRY BROWN

Larry Brown

Running back Larry Brown was so fast that the first time he tried the Lombardi Sweep, he collided with the guards.

"It was scary," he admitted. "That probably had something to do with my quickness."

Brown only played eight seasons, the last three sort of a slow exit, before giving way to John Riggins. But from 1969-72, Brown was one of the more feared runners in the game in making four straight Pro Bowls. Quickness was the key. His linemen just needed to create a sliver of an opening and Brown would slice through.

"Larry didn't rely on power," said Redskins receiver Charley Taylor. "His thing would be getting there quicker than the defense."

Said quarterback Billy Kilmer: "Larry was never offside, but he was instantly on the ball and one of the quickest to the hole."

Assistant coach Ted Marchibroda called Brown, "pound for pound the toughest guy I've seen in 30 years of coaching."

That may have been the reason behind Brown's greatness, but also his undoing. Coach George Allen used Brown time after time over four seasons with 237 carries the lightest load. Brown retired as the Redskins' all-time rushing leader with 5,875 yards, a total that was later eclipsed by Riggins, but the pounding surely ended his career prematurely.

"It probably did," Brown admitted, "but I guess the average career span is 3 1/2 to 4 1/2 years so I was fortunate to play longer. During that era, all the players sacrificed their bodies. It just seemed because I was running the ball a lot it was more noticeable."

Said Taylor: "If Larry needed three yards, he would probably throw his body in there to get three yards."

Defensive tackle Diron Talbert remembered Brown as "Hell on wheels and just as nasty. I've never seen anyone work as hard in practice as he did on every single running play. He used to put a white towel down 25 yards from the line of scrimmage, and if we had a running play, he would sprint to that towel every time."

Vince Lombardi only coached Brown during his 1969 rookie season, but made a profound impact on the runner. Lombardi noticed Brown was late off the snap count. It turned out Brown didn't hear well in one ear, and Lombardi had a hearing aid installed in his helmet.

"It would transfer sound from my bad ear to my good ear," Brown said. "I didn't have [a hearing aid] in college and no one noticed, but Lombardi did during films."

After allegedly fumbling during practice — which Brown denies — Lombardi ordered him to carry the ball everywhere he went. To dinner. To meetings. To bed.

"He thought I fumbled and I told him I didn't in front of the team," Brown said. "He didn't like it. He told me I must carry a football around with me for a week. He was an extremely tough coach, but also very fair. He was a field general like General [George] Patton."

Brown's greatest season came in 1972 when he rushed for 1,216 yards — including six 100-yard games — in helping lead the Redskins to Super Bowl VII. He gained 191 yards on 29 carries with two touchdowns against the New York Giants at Yankee Stadium.

"When I scored a touchdown, somebody threw a can of beer at me in the end zone, and it wasn't even my brand," Brown said. "Things like that really get your adrenaline going."

That Brown has never elected to the Hall of Fame still bothers many from the Over The Hill Gang. Kilmer said "He was the best all-around back I ever played with. He should be in the Hall of Fame."

Brown said, "I find it very shocking too, but why did it take [Baltimore tight end] John Mackey so long to get into the Hall of Fame? Sportswriters vote for the Hall of Fame, and we should have former players and coaches voting, too. Somebody has to stand up [during elections] and fight for you."

Just as Brown did for the Redskins.

As A Redskin

Position: Running back.

Years: 1969-76.

Stats: 5,875 yards rushing, 238 receptions for 2,485 yards, 55 touchdowns.

Greatest season: Gained 1,216 yards in 12 games in 1972.

Honors: Pro Bowl, 1969-72; Player of the Year, 1972.

Today: Real estate executive, Potomac, Md.

KEN HOUSTON MAKES THE MOST MEMORABLE TACKLE IN REDSKINS HISTORY.

The Greatest Tackle

Redskins 14, Cowboys 7

They thought he was in. Check that. They *knew* he was in. Dallas running back Walt Garrison grabbed the fourth-down pass at the goal line and needed only a foot or so to tie the game, send it into overtime and deflate the Redskins with a last-second touchdown. No one corralled the 6-foot, 205-pound Garrison in this situation. The guy wrestled steers for crying out loud.

Nearly 55,000 fans at RFK Stadium clammed up, awaiting the bad news from the officials. Any second now, those arms would be raised skyward, signaling a touchdown. So they watched in silence, as if viewing an accident site. Even the Redskins feared the worst. In this battle for first place, overtime beckoned.

"When he caught the ball," said Redskins defensive tackle Bill Brundige, "I said, 'That's it.' Garrison was very, very difficult to stop cold. He could twist, he would turn. So when he caught the ball, I knew from where I was and where he was, if he wasn't across the goal line, he was right at it. I just knew that was it."

Enter Ken Houston.

The Redskins strong safety, read the play perfectly. Dallas had run it before in this game and, on this fourth-and-goal from the 6 with 24 seconds to play, the Cowboys called it again. Quarterback Craig Morton rolled right and Garrison swung out of the backfield and planted himself on that side.

On the play, Houston, the back of his feet touching the goal line, and free safety Brig Owens played a 'combination C' coverage on the tight end and running back. When the tight end, and first option, Jean Fugett released, Owens covered him.

Many times, Houston would be on the tight end.

"I called the defense and [Houston] said to call another," said linebacker Chris Hanburger. "That was one of the few times I listened to someone else and it put him in perfect position. That was Ken's call the whole way. It was a defense that instead of covering a tight end to the inside, it allowed Ken to sit there and pick up the fullback."

That left Garrison — and a spot in Redskins lore — to Houston.

Morton pump faked, igniting the charge by Houston. When the ball was thrown, Garrison jumped and Houston raced at him.

Before Garrison was able to land both feet on the ground, Houston wrapped his arms around him. He yanked Garrison, whose right leg reached for the goal line, backwards and disabled any shot at forward momentum.

Eventually, Garrison abandoned the notion of scoring himself, scanned the field for a teammate and lateraled the ball. But that didn't work either as it was smothered by Redskins around the 5-yard line. That clinched a 14-7 Washington victory in the teams' first meeting since the Redskins' 1972 NFC Championship victory. Dallas wanted revenge, instead it got more heartache and dropped to 3-1, same as Washington.

"I thought [Garrison] was going to step in because I knew where he was," Houston said. "He was trying to lateral the ball and I was yelling for Brig to help me. And it was like I was talking on the telephone. That's how quiet it was. I'll never forget that. It was like I was the only voice on the field and everyone else was holding their breath and waiting for it to happen. No one said a word. Then when everyone realized what had happened, it got louder and louder and louder."

After the game, all Garrison would say is, "I was close, very close."

Who would figure that Garrison, who finished his career in 1974 with 3,886 yards rushing and another 1,794 yards receiving, would be denied?

Cornerback Pat Fischer, who was covering "Bullet" Bob Hayes, for one.

After the ball was thrown and Garrison jumped, Fischer figured Houston had the advantage.

"If his feet were on the ground when Kenny hit him, I don't know if Kenny could have stopped him from getting that one yard," Fischer said. "But when his feet were in the air, Kenny was so strong that when his feet

REDSKINS 14, COWBOYS 7					
	1	2	3	4	Total
Cowboys	0	7	0	0	7
Redskins	0	0	0	14	14

SECOND QUARTER
D — Stowe 15 pass from Staubach (Fritsch kick), D 7-0

FOURTH QUARTER
W — Taylor 1 pass from Jurgensen (Knight kick), 7-7
W — Owens 26 interception return (Knight kick), W 14-7

came down, Kenny had him stopped."

Owens said, "We would talk about how you had to get [Garrison's] cleats out of the ground to stop him. There have been plenty of great tackles, but that one was such a timely tackle."

Houston: "If he had the ball and got both feet on the ground, it would have been a tossup. I would have had to hit him hard enough to knock him back and that's very difficult. I would probably be able to do that two out of 10 times."

But he did it, six months after arriving in a trade for five players. Houston had validated the deal with the Oilers. It also helped him ease the pain over his departure from his home state.

In 1972, Houston dislocated a toe — against Dallas — and didn't have a spectacular year. The following offseason, the Oilers wanted him to sign a three-year contract, which was two more than he was willing to accept. Eventually, the Oilers had enough. But the Redskins, particularly coach George Allen, liked him from the start. That play cemented their feelings.

"I remember George saying that one play was enough for the deal," Houston said. "Guys welcomed me from the beginning, but now they knew I had come to play football."

Houston made other big plays against Dallas. In 1974, Houston returned a punt 58 yards for a touchdown, the only such play in his career, as the Redskins won, 28-21. Houston was not the regular punt returner — Larry Jones was, but he was injured. (Later in that game, Houston fumbled a punt. Allen never stuck him back there again).

A year later, Houston intercepted a Roger Staubach pass in overtime to set up the game-winning score in a 30-24 victory. And, in 1978, Houston picked off a pass in the end zone intended for receiver Drew Pearson to preserve a 9-5 win.

"It seemed like when I played Dallas, I got on another level," said Houston. "I really got caught up in the George Allen hype. You did not want to come home to [Texas] having lost to the Cowboys. I have a picture of me intercepting a ball against Dallas. The ball was in the air, I saw it and I remember jumping extremely high - I think my feet were alongside the guy's head. I don't know how I jumped that high or why I jumped that high."

But none of those plays compared to the Garrison tackle. Houston — who lives in the Houston suburb of Kingwood — said he is reminded of that play at least two or three times a week, usually from Dallas fans who lost money on the game. Others remember it as a classic Monday Night Football moment.

Even Garrison, whom Houston has seen a half-dozen times since, can't forget the tackle. He asked Houston to send him a picture of the game-saving play.

Defensive tackle Diron Talbert understands why such a fuss is still being made.

"That may be the defensive play of the century," said Talbert.

Ironically, Houston was initially trying to intercept the ball. Had he succeeded, he might have raced the length of the field for a touchdown. With the Oilers, Houston had a knack for doing just that, setting an NFL record with nine such scores.

"I thought I could intercept the ball," Houston said. "And I was going to step between Garrison and the ball, but I couldn't get there. He landed on one foot and tried to step in with the other and I picked him up."

Houston is convinced if he had picked off that pass and returned it for six points, that game would not be remembered as it is today. He also says that tackle didn't win the game. That honor belonged to Owens.

Houston saved a touchdown; Owens scored one.

Owens' heroics came moments after the Redskins had finally pulled even in this defensive struggle. Neither team scored until 49 seconds remained in the first half when Staubach (who later left the game with a severe charley horse) passed to receiver Otto Stowe for a 15-yard score, punctuating a 19-play drive. Washington marched right back, but Curt Knight missed a 44-yard field goal try as the half ended. It was one of three misses in the game for the struggling Knight.

In the first half, Dallas recorded 13 first downs to Washington's three. The Redskins were lucky to still be in the game and might not have been if not for a blocked field goal (by Ron McDole) and a blocked punt (by Bill Malinchak).

Defensive end Verlon Biggs came through in similar fashion on the Cowboys' first drive of the third quarter. After Dallas drove to the 16, two sacks stalled the drive and Toni Fritsch attempted a 38-yard field goal. But Biggs knocked it down for the Redskins' third blocked kick of the night.

But the Redskins continued a troubling habit and didn't capitalize. Later in the third quarter, Knight stumbled again as he missed a 30-yarder. Two years earlier, Knight had made the Pro Bowl. But he couldn't make anything in 1973 as he missed nine of his first 12 attempts. With Allen's defensive emphasis, every point was necessary.

"One frustrating thing during the Allen years was, we had great defenses but we didn't blow them out on offense," Brundige said. "A lot of times, the defense had to win the game."

So they did just that. First, however, the Redskins' offense finally managed to score. After the defense forced a punt late in the fourth quarter, Washington took over at its own 43. Quarterback Sonny Jurgensen went to work. The veteran completed four passes — two to favorite receiver Charley Taylor for 24 yards — moving the Redskins to the Dallas 18. Taylor then drew a pass interference penalty in the end zone and the

Brig Owens' interception and ensuing touchdown gives the Redskins the lead.

Redskins had a first-and-goal at the 1.

Three plays later, Jurgensen, stepped back one foot and lobbed a pass to Taylor in the corner of the end zone. Taylor outjumped the defenders, caught the ball and, after Knight's extra point, the game was tied with 3:39 remaining.

The tie didn't last long. Three plays to be exact.

On Dallas's next series, Morton dropped back to pass on third-and-9 at the Cowboy 19. He spotted tight end Billy Joe DuPree in the right flat, but Owens read the play. He raced in front of DuPree, grabbed the pass and, 26 yards later, snapped the tie. Dallas answered with its final drive, which included a 17-yard pass from Morton to Garrison on fourth-and-one to the Washington 4.

Four plays later, history was made.

The Redskins went on to finish 10-4 and lost at Minnesota in the first round of the playoffs. Dallas, which got revenge with a 27-7 win on Dec. 9, ended with the same record. The Cowboys also lost to Minnesota, but not until the NFC Championship.

As for Houston, he led the team in interceptions with six and was named to the Pro Bowl. So, too, were Hanburger, Taylor, center Len Hauss and kick returner Herb Mul-Key.

But 1973 will long be remembered for Houston's tackle.

"It was just frozen in time," said Brundige, who ran a stunt on the play with end McDole.

Brundige pressured Morton, jumped to block the pass then turned around and watched.

"When [Garrison] jumped up, it seemed like he hung there forever. He caught the ball and everyone just stopped like that's it. It was one of those classic mano a mano confrontations. Houston and Garrison. And Kenny got him," Brundige said.

KEN HOUSTON

Ken Houston

This couldn't be the same guy. Could it? Ken Houston is too nice, too peaceful. When his mind gets frazzled, he seeks refuge on a golf course, soaking in deer sightings and admiring trees while playing solo. This guy frightened receivers?

But this doesn't sound like a peaceful man:

"You wanted to put [receivers] out of the game," said Houston, who won numerous civic awards in the NFL. "You wanted to see the ball go one way and him go another."

In other words, as split as Houston's personality.

"Ken was Dr. Jekyll and Mr. Hyde," said defensive tackle Bill Brundige. "He didn't smoke, drink, swear. He was a Christian fellow, had a super-intelligent wife. He was the nicest guy you'd ever want to meet in your entire life. But when he got on the field and put those elbow pads on, he was vicious."

Houston is best remembered for his last-second tackle of Walt Garrison in a 14-7 win over Dallas in 1973. But more savage hits defined his play. Not only was Houston the best Redskins safety ever, he was named to the NFL's Team of the 1970s. Houston was selected to 12 straight Pro Bowls, more than any other safety. Seven of those came with the Redskins, who acquired him in a five-for-one trade with the Houston Oilers, who didn't like it that he was a players' union representative.

That 1973 deal was a steal for the Redskins, who gave up offensive tackle Jim Snowden, tight end Mack Alston, defensive back Jeff Severson, receiver Clifton McNeil and defensive end Mike Fanucci to get Houston.

The trade stung Houston.

"It was traumatic," he remembered. Then, when he arrived for his first camp, "[Coach] George Allen ran me on second team. Then [free safety] Roosevelt Taylor broke his arm, they moved Brig Owens over there and put me in at strong safety. [Before that], I was thinking, 'I've been All-Pro five years . . . ' I didn't think it would last, but then I realized George's philosophy: You don't lose a position. Somebody takes it."

Houston seized it and held the job until 1980 when Tony Peters came along. Houston retired after that season with one disappointment - coach Jack Pardee didn't play him in his final game at RFK Stadium, a 16-13 win on Dec. 13 against the Giants. Ironically, it was Ken Houston Day.

"I don't know exactly what happened," Houston said. "I remember Jack saying I would have a hard time covering the tight end. I couldn't buy that. My career had been too good to dwell on those last few games.

But it bothered me. It bothered me big time."

The 6-foot-3, 198-pound Houston was drafted in the ninth round in 1967 out of Prairie View (Tex.) — where he played linebacker. He quit twice during his rookie camp with the Oilers, convinced he had no chance. Also, because of his religious upbringing, Houston struggled with the idea of playing a game on Sundays.

Some NFL receivers, who called him dirty, probably wish he hadn't returned to stalk them with his forearm smashings.

"He would hit someone and pop their helmet 15 feet," said Washington defensive tackle Dave Butz.

"I was not a dirty player," said Houston, who coached in the NFL for five years, college for three and high school for four more. "I was very aggressive and I didn't take any cheap shots. I would hit a guy hard and I would clothesline him. But clotheslining was legal. They didn't like it, but that's the way it was."

And what did it feel like when he nailed a receiver?

"It was just like I had a hole-in-one," Houston said. "You didn't get those kind of licks often, but those were the kinds of hits you'd go in on Tuesday and have them run the film back. You play all day to get a shot like that."

But that wasn't the only side to Houston.

"I learned about being a professional football player from Ken Houston," said Redskins linebacker Mel Kaufman. "If I had to pick a role model for my kids, it would be Ken."

As A Redskin

Position: Safety.

Years: 1973-80.

Stats: 24 interceptions; started 99 straight games from 1973-79.

Greatest season: Led team with six interceptions and justified 5-for-1 trade with goal-line, game-saving tackle of Dallas' Walt Garrison in 1973.

Honors: Pro Bowl, 1973-79; Hall of Fame, 1986.

Today: Counselor at Terrell Alternative School in Houston.

BRIG OWENS

Brig Owens

Brig Owens didn't plan on playing 13 NFL seasons. He had his degree from the University of Cincinnati and his future planned.

"I never thought I would be able to play as long as I did," Owens said. "I told my wife, 'If I can just play three years and earn enough money, I'll go ahead and coach high school because this game is not really fun, it's all business.' I was prepared just to play three years, but three years went to four and four to five to get vested in the pension plan and all of a sudden, I'm playing my 13th year."

Just as surprising was where Owens played those years. He was drafted by Dallas in the seventh round as a quarterback in 1965 after finishing fourth in the nation in total offense as a senior at Cincinnati. But a few days into training camp, Cowboys coach Tom Landry switched him to safety.

"I had never played defense before, so I began studying opposing players really hard," Owens said. "That was how I was going to succeed."

Owens didn't succeed with the Cowboys. He spent the year on their taxi squad before being traded to Washington for Jim Steffen.

"The trade was the best thing that happened in my career," Owens said. "Dallas was a very impersonal organization. There were a lot of racial problems in the city. I couldn't eat in certain places. There were certain places I couldn't live. We were supposed to be ambassadors for the city and we should have been treated that way. I complained and I think that started some of my problems with the Cowboys. I was glad to leave Dallas. To be able to show the Cowboys I could play meant a lot to me. It was special for me to beat Dallas."

Owens was welcomed to Washington as a younger brother by the team's first black player, Bobby Mitchell, and quickly immersed himself in community affairs. Owens also formed a then-rare inter-racial bond with another young student of the game, tight end Jerry Smith.

"Jerry and I would talk about certain situations," Owens said. "I would talk about how tight ends played me or about other defensive backs' weaknesses. He would do the same for me, talking about other tight ends' moves. We were always strategizing."

Owens' shining moment during his first year in Washington came on Nov. 27 when he returned an interception 60 yards for a touchdown and took back a fumble 62 yards for another in a record-breaking 72-41 victory over the New York Giants. Owens intercepted two more passes that day in an amazing performance.

The Redskins, who had endured nine straight losing seasons, finished at .500 during Owens' first year and went on to record eight winning seasons during his tenure. Owens played in all 154 games during his first 11 Washington seasons. Along the way, he picked off 36 passes, a club record until Darrell Green broke it in 1995. And Owens' 686 yards on interception returns are still easily the most by a Redskin.

But Owens never took his success for granted. He always remembered the advice he received from veteran Dallas cornerback Don Bishop during his rookie year.

"Bishop told me, 'Take care of your body and it will take care of you,' " Owens said. "I always made sure I was in shape year-round."

The safeties the coaches brought to training camp each summer to challenge Owens, who never made a Pro Bowl, could match his athletic ability. But they didn't have Owens' mind.

"Brig was an extremely smart player," safety Richie Petitbon said. "You're talking about a player who didn't have the greatest physical tools, but he tuned into the game. It's assumed everyone in the pros does this [knowing where your teammates are and reading patterns] but that's not the case. Most try to get by on athletic ability. Those are the ones that don't last."

Owens was like a coach on the field.

"Brig was in [coach] George Allen's head," said Hall of Famer Ken Houston, Owens' partner at safety from 1973-76. "He knew exactly what George wanted done."

Naturally, the brainy Owens was prepared for the inevitable end to his career. Elected player representative by his teammates, Owens became a member of the negotiating committee for the Washington-based NFL Players Association.

Owens attended law school at night and in the offseasons. After his retirement, he spent five years with the NFLPA before forming his own sports management firm. Owens has stayed in the game by representing such Redskins stars as Art Monk and Wilber Marshall. And of course, he still roots for the Redskins.

"Being traded to Washington, a city that truly loved its team, totally changed my life on and off the field," Owens said.

As A Redskin

Position: Safety.

Years: 1966-77.

Stats: 36 interceptions, club-record 686 yards in interception returns.

Greatest season: 7 interceptions and 2 TDs in 1966.

Today: Partner, sports management firm of Bennett and Owens, Washington D.C.

SONNY JURGENSEN LAUNCHES A PASS IN HIS "SUPER BOWL."

The Redhead's Last Stand

Redskins 20, Dolphins 17

For 18 years, quarterback Sonny Jurgensen dragged his aching body back onto the field for more punishment. Fans sometimes booed him. Defenses often bruised him — surgical scars provided a roadmap of his career. Yet he endured. All Jurgensen wanted was to play football. And all he wanted beyond that was a Super Bowl appearance.

In 1972, the Redskins got that chance. But Jurgensen's body had betrayed him again. In the season's eighth game, he tore his Achilles' tendon. This time, the mental pain equaled the physical aches. There would be no Super Bowl for one of the game's best-ever passers.

Instead, while his team played the Miami Dolphins in Super Bowl VII, Jurgensen sat in a Los Angeles Coliseum coaches box, alone with his thoughts and his crutches. On the field, the Redskins, whom he had made exciting for years with his right arm, stumbled to a 14-7 loss with quarterback Billy Kilmer.

"That was the most disappointing thing in my life," Jurgensen said. I was standing on the field before the game and [Miami coach] Don Shula walks by and came over to me and said, 'I know how hard you worked to get here. I know how disappointing this must be. And I'm sorry you're not going to be able to play in this thing because it would be a better game if you were.'

"I always felt we would have won if I'd had the opportunity to play. But I was hurt. If they had just let me talk to Billy [during the game], we might have won. They kept me off the sidelines. They didn't want me to be a part of it. Maybe [coach George Allen] felt I was a distraction."

Two years later, Allen felt Jurgensen was the answer against the Dolphins. It was the first time the teams had met in a regular season game since the Super Bowl and the Redskins hadn't forgotten their missed title shot.

After a rousing win over Dallas in the 1972 NFC Championship Game, the players wanted time to bask in their glory. But Allen, wedded to routine, wanted to maintain his team's workout schedule despite a two-week layoff before the Super Bowl.

"After we beat the Cowboys, the town was in chaos and it was just a tremendous feeling," said defensive tackle Bill Brundige. "We had a meeting that Tuesday morning and George said, 'Enough of that. Now it's on to the Super Bowl.' What we needed was another three or four days to reflect. He said we're going to act like we're playing on Sunday so we went through a full week's practice. Instead of playing on Sunday, we flew to Los Angeles. At that point, we were ready to play. We weren't ready to play the following week."

Receiver Charley Taylor remembered, "We lost that game on that Thursday [before the Super Bowl]. We couldn't do anything wrong [in practice]. Everything was clicking. No balls were dropped, nothing. We sat back and said, 'Let's get it on.' Now you have to wait another three days. You're human. Guys got restless and did some things they shouldn't have done. There were a couple of conflicts.

"During the game we were like, 'Wait a minute, we were hitting this pass against the zone on Thursday. We can't get the damn thing over the safety's head now.' "

And as Taylor said: "We didn't have the Redhead, and that put a little strain on us right there."

REDSKINS 20, DOLPHINS 17					
	1	2	3	4	Total
Dolphins	7	0	3	7	17
Redskins	0	0	3	17	20

FIRST QUARTER
M — Ginn 6 run (Yepremian kick), M 7-0

THIRD QUARTER
M — Yepremian 32 FG, M 10-0
W — Moseley 40 FG, M 10-3

FOURTH QUARTER
W — Jefferson 33 pass from Jurgensen (Moseley kick), 10-10
W — Moseley 41 FG, W 13-10
M — Twilley 13 pass from Griese (Yepremian kick), M 17-13
W — L. Smith 6 pass from Jurgensen (Moseley kick), W 20-17

But they had the redheaded Jurgensen for the rematch in 1974. No one could know it would be the last big win of Jurgensen's Hall of Fame career. And he would do it in style in front of 54,395 fans, thrilling everyone from Allen to 7-year-old Eric Jurgensen — in attendance for the first time ever to watch his dad.

First, though, Jurgensen had to get the start. Kilmer had been starting that season, but the team was only 2-2 following a 28-17 loss to Cincinnati on Oct. 6. Washington's fans clung to the "I Love Sonny" and "I Love Billy" battle. The quarterbacks themselves never let it get personal, even though their rotation lasted four years. Both only wanted to win.

That's all Allen wanted as well. Kilmer, who ranked first in the NFC in passing, allegedly had a bruised leg and Allen used that as the reason for the switch. But the Redskins' offense had been inconsistent all season.

During the week, after Allen had told Jurgensen of the move, he had a chat with his quarterback, with whom he had often clashed.

"I remember George Allen saying to me, 'You know, a lot of coaches wouldn't do this, start a 40-year-old,'" Jurgensen said. "I said, 'Well, if you want to win, you will.'"

The players, though staunch Kilmer supporters because of his leadership, loved Jurgensen. They also knew he was still the better passer.

Kilmer had struggled against Miami's two-deep zone in the Super Bowl. And with the Dolphins concentrating on stopping running back Larry Brown, Kilmer needed to pass the Redskins to victory. It didn't happen.

That's why Jurgensen wanted to be on the sidelines for that game. Jurgensen figured his conversations with Kilmer would have helped. After all, Jurgensen was better at picking apart zone coverages than Kilmer or most quarterbacks for that matter.

"You had to have the arm to beat that, someone to have that touch to pass it in those cracks in the defense," Taylor said. "We knew Sonny would make time for [the patterns] to develop and that's all we needed. Billy could see it, but he was just a step too soon with it."

But Jurgensen's return wasn't the only reason the players were excited. Allen, a master motivator with his bulletin board of press clippings, even closed practices to the media that week.

Safety Brig Owens recalled, "We had something to pay back. George was talking about it all week."

Jurgensen, who had appeared in only two games as a substitute that season, was cheered wildly when introduced. But it was the Redskins' top-ranked defense that kept them in the game, even though it allowed Miami to drive for a touchdown after the opening kickoff. Those were the only points of the first half. Three Jurgensen interceptions — against one of the league's best defenses despite its "No-Name" moniker — caused fans to wonder if he was finished.

One of the interceptions was tipped, but one was Jurgensen's fault and it was critical. With one minute remaining in the first half, receiver Roy Jefferson broke open in the end zone. But cornerback Tim Foley picked off the ball.

"When you live by the pass," Jurgensen said. "You're going to die by it at times."

Special teams sparked the Redskins in the second half. Larry Jones returned the kickoff to his own 43, but Washington stalled on the Miami 29 when a fourth-and-one run was stuffed. For the next eight minutes, Miami — playing minus running back Mercury Morris and receiver Paul Warfield, out with injuries — drove downfield and added a 32-yard Garo Yepremian field goal for a 10-0 lead.

Jones then returned the kickoff 57 yards, which led to a 40-yard Mark Moseley field goal. On the ensuing kickoff, Dennis Johnson forced a fumble, Brad Dusek recovered at the Miami 33 and the Redskins were rolling. Jurgensen kept it going, firing a perfect pass to Jefferson, running a post pattern, for the game-tying score. Nineteen seconds earlier, Washington had trailed 10-0. Now it was tied.

"Sonny was like magic," said offensive tackle George Starke. "He was like Michael Jordan. Everyone else was playing football; Sonny was playing something else."

It took one drive to untie the score. But it was a costly drive. Brown was ejected for fighting after he felt cornerback Henry Stuckey had hit him after he had run out of bounds at the Miami 30. The setback — Washington was also assessed a 15-yard penalty — was temporary. A 19-yard pass to Jefferson set up a 41-yard Moseley field goal for a 13-10 Redskins' lead.

Then came rally time. First up, Miami, which had been throttled all day by Washington's defense that held

Larry Smith (38) helps carry Washington to victory over Miami.

fullback Larry Csonka to 58 yards on 18 carries.

"We looked at film of the Super Bowl over and over," said Brundige. "It was hard to bring Csonka down. They had a fake toss and would run a trap inside that hurt us badly. We stuffed that [in the rematch]."

But after Moseley missed a 45-yarder with five minutes to play, the Dolphins drove for the go-ahead score. Griese connected with receiver Nat Moore for a 48-yard gain to the Washington 24 on a third-and-10. After getting another first down, Miami was faced with a third-and-11 from the 13. But a blitz by cornerback Mike Bass failed as Griese delivered the ball just before getting hit and connected with receiver Howard Twilley for a touchdown. Twilley was wide open in the area Bass had vacated.

Now it was Washington's turn. With 1:44 to play — and after a 32-yard kickoff return by Herb Mul-Key — the Redskins began the game-winning drive on their own 40.

"The great part of that drive was Sonny came in and he was having a ball," said fullback Larry Smith. "He was laughing. He had so much confidence that we were going to win. You could tell he was enjoying it. That's what he liked."

Jurgensen said, "It was fun. God, I was playing in my 18th year. It was fun to be in a game like that and to have that opportunity against them."

The first five plays of the drive went like this: Six-yard pass to running back Moses Denson; 10-yard pass to tight end Jerry Smith; four-yard pass to Taylor; 18-yard pass to Taylor; 16-yard pass to Jefferson. The Redskins had a first down at the Miami 6 with 28 seconds remaining. Then came the only incompletion of the drive, a pass to Larry Smith, running a slant across the middle. Linebacker Doug Swift tackled Smith before the ball arrived, but the officials let it go.

The same play was called. This time, Smith made the catch and stretched the ball into the end zone as linebacker Nick Buoniconti crashed into him. The Dolphins protested that Smith never crossed the goal line. The officials disagreed. The Redskins won, 20-17.

"When I landed, I wasn't in the end zone, but the ball had broken the plane," Smith said. "At least that's what the officials said. I thought I had it, but it was close."

For Smith, it was his only hurrah with Washington. He had played that game with a stress fracture in his left foot and his left hand was also broken. The next week versus the New York Giants he broke his left leg and his Redskins career ended in the same year it began after he arrived in a trade with the Rams.

Few would miss Smith. But many would miss Jurgensen. The Redhead played in two more games as injuries — and Allen — forced him back to the bench. After the season, Jurgensen retired after being told by Allen he would be a backup at best.

But the Miami victory sent him out in style. Jurgensen finished that game 26-of-39 for 303 yards and two touchdowns.

"That," Jurgensen said, "was my Super Bowl."

photo by Arnie Sachs and the staff of Consolidated News Photo

CHRIS HANBURGER

Chris Hanburger

Maybe it was the hours of game film that linebacker Chris Hanburger watched on Friday nights in his living room, just hours before viewing them again the following morning with the team. Perhaps it was the four or five daily meetings with Redskins coach George Allen. Either way, Hanburger was ready one afternoon against the St. Louis Cardinals.

"As the center snaps the ball, before it even gets to the quarterback, Chris is sprinting across the line of scrimmage," recalled defensive tackle Bill Brundige. "As the halfback gets the ball, Chris tackles him. On the next play, Chris buzzes to the outside before the quarterback gets the ball. I asked him after the game 'Chris, how in the world did you know that play before the quarterback got the ball?' It was just by looking at the way the halfback was in his crouch, looking at the linemen and the whole deal. He just had an instinct that was uncanny."

Hanburger played 14 seasons with the Redskins, including nine Pro Bowl years. He wasn't the biggest linebacker. Indeed, Hanburger often taped a pair of 2 1/2-pound weights to his chest during weekly weigh-ins to avoid being fined for sometimes falling below 205 pounds.

But Hanburger compensated by knowing opposing offenses. Brundige said Hanburger could anticipate better than anyone. But that wasn't really it. Hanburger just studied more than most. He would watch game films endlessly, looking for a small tip off like which way a player would lean. That's how he knew where the ball was going and why Allen made him the defensive signal-caller in 1973 after Jack Pardee retired.

"If a halfback put his head down, it didn't always mean he would carry the ball, and if it were up that he would pick up the blitz and you should expect pass," Hanburger said. "But it gives you a mental edge on what they're trying to do. Down and distance tell you a lot."

OK, maybe those long nights of watching film sometimes were only long enough to open the canisters to ensure Allen wasn't testing his dedication by switching footage. But Hanburger and Allen became successful despite a love-hate relationship because both were too intense to let the other seem more dedicated.

"Chris was a George Allen-type of player," said defensive tackle Diron Talbert. "He and Chris didn't always get along because of the long drawn-out meetings. But Chris got as much out of George Allen as George got out of Chris."

Said Hanburger: "When I started calling defenses, George drove me crazy. I would meet with him before the team meetings and during defensive meetings, then before practice and after practice. At nights, he would call me at home. I could almost pick up the phone and say 'Hi, coach' because I knew it was him. But if that's what it took, then that's what it took."

Hanburger stood apart from his teammates off the field, too. He was called a loner on the Over The Hill Gang that was legendary for its closeness among veterans. Safety Ken Houston called him "a different breed of cat."

Hanburger admits it was true. Still is. He lived in Upper Marlboro, Md., an hour away from Redskin Park when most players lived near the Herndon, Va., facility. Being sociable while knocking people on their tails is something he never mastered.

"I didn't hang around with them," Hanburger said of his teammates. "I've never been a sociable person. I can't stand to eat out. I can't remember the last movie I went to. I know I'm a loner. It doesn't bother me at all."

Standing out or standing alone . . . it made no difference to Hanburger.

As A Redskin

Position: Linebacker.

Years: 1965-78.

Stats: 19 interceptions, 12 fumble recoveries, 5 touchdowns.

Greatest season: Made 4 interceptions and 1 touchdown in 1972.

Honors: Pro Bowl, 1966-69, 1972-76; NFC Defensive Player of the Year in 1972.

Today: Auto parts manager, Upper Marlboro, Md.

photo by Arnie Sachs and the staff of Consolidated News Photo

PAT FISCHER

Pat Fischer

Even now, Pat Fischer is greeted with curious stares. That's only natural. Fischer, who retired in 1977, never looked like an NFL player when he was one and certainly doesn't resemble one who lasted 17 years. Aren't ex-stars bigger than 5-foot-9 and 170 pounds?

Not in this case. But that doesn't stop people from asking, with disbelief, if he played.

"I say no," Fischer said. "It's too hard to explain and it's not worth it. Even when I played, people would ask that question and I would think, 'What do you want me to do, run around and prove it?' "

A better question is, how did he last so long? He wasn't fast (though he always covered Dallas' Bullet Bob Hayes) and he was a 17th round draft pick in 1961 out of Nebraska. His vision stunk (20/200). However, Fischer was one of Washington's best-ever cornerbacks after he arrived in 1968 following seven years with St. Louis. While with the Cardinals, Fischer was the first NFL cornerback to play the bump-and-run.

His former teammates call him feisty. He had to be. Fischer's assignments ranged from covering a 6-9 receiver like Philadelphia's Harold Carmichael to tackling a bulldozing running back like Cleveland's Jim Brown.

Redskins safety Richie Petitbon remembers a playoff game in 1972 against Green Bay when Fischer tackled 6-foot-1, 225-pound running back John Brockington for losses three or four times.

"Pat's eyesight wasn't that good," Petitbon said. "I don't think he realized how big that guy was. He was just dumping him on his [butt]. It was a tremendous performance. His was the classic story of the will to win."

But Fischer never worried about smacking into bigger players. After all, he'd been doing it since the third grade in St. Edwards, Neb., as his four older brothers had done.

Fischer didn't think about what he couldn't do. Rather, he attacked a situation by reducing it to something doable.

"If you say to me, you have to tackle Jimmy Brown, well all I have to do is attack one side and get one of his legs off the ground and by that time, I'll have a lot of help," Fischer said. "It's the same with a tall receiver. We're not playing basketball. I could hit him and do lots of things. My job was to not let him catch the ball. If he does, try to knock him down."

"Pat would hit [Carmichael] in the nose or throat and frustrate him," safety Brig Owens said. "That's how he played big receivers."

Ex-teammates chuckle when discussing Fischer. Before games — after downing a pot of coffee — he smoked until he was introduced, then chucked his cigarette in the dugout and ran onto the field. On cold days, defensive tackle Diron Talbert said, "the smoke would come through his earholes and it looked like his head was on fire." Not true, Fischer said about the last part.

Defensive tackle Bill Brundige remembered Fischer placing the gooey substance, stick-em, in his mouth. Fischer said it happened only once. But it was enough.

"He'd be in the huddle and you'd look at him and he'd be drooling out of his mouth because of that damn stick-em," Brundige recalled.

Preparation and self-control keyed Fischer's success and film study became a ritual by his third NFL season. That helped him pick off 27 passes with Washington and 56 overall.

"I can run reels in my mind today of Bob Hayes or Cleveland's Gary Collins running pass patterns," Fischer said. "I can see every step, that's how many times I would view those films. I can still see them leaving the huddle. I can see how they line up and I can see their first step from the line of scrimmage."

Fischer never had a major injury during the season. He retired having played more games at cornerback (213) than anyone else in league history.

"Pat was tough as nails," strong safety Ken Houston said. "He was a special breed."

COACH JOE GIBBS

Joe Gibbs

Joe Gibbs still gets a kick out of imagining Redskins owner Jack Kent Cooke's reaction when general manager Bobby Beathard suggested he hire San Diego's 40-year-old offensive coordinator Gibbs as his coach.

"I can hear Mr. Cooke saying, 'Joe who?' " Gibbs said, imitating the imperial Cooke's voice before starting to laugh at the thought.

"Joe who?" was no laughing matter in October 1981. Cooke had fired coach Jack Pardee the year before after the team's first losing season in a decade. Gibbs, who had never been a head coach on any level, was 0-5 and wondered if Cooke was going to fire him.

But Beathard and Cooke both stood behind Gibbs, who reworked the offense to give John Riggins the ball more in a one-back, two tight end scheme. The Redskins won eight of their final 11 games and a year later captured their first Super Bowl title as Riggins ran to glory.

Gibbs went on to win two more Super Bowls while guiding Washington to eight playoff berths in 12 years and posting the third-best record for any coach with at least 100 victories. If not for a missed 29-yard field goal by Chip Lohmiller in the 1988 finale, Gibbs never would have had a losing season. No wonder he was elected to the Pro Football Hall of Fame the first year he was nominated.

"Joe had the same characteristics he had as a player as a coach," said Don Coryell, Gibbs' coach at San Diego State (1961-63) and his boss with the St. Louis Cardinals (1973-77) and the Chargers (1979-80). "He was intelligent, versatile, feisty and hard-nosed."

And a fierce competitor.

"My burning desire from the time I was a young kid was to compete and beat somebody," said Gibbs, a one-time senior national racquetball champion who went on to own a successful NASCAR team.

An average college player, Gibbs kept those competitive fires burning through coaching stints at his alma mater, then Florida State, Southern Cal and Arkansas. He hit the NFL with St. Louis at 32 and moved on to Tampa Bay and San Diego before coming to Washington.

Hall of Fame receiver Charlie Joiner, who played under Gibbs in San Diego, marveled that he would spend all night in the office to develop a single play.

All that effort paid off on Sundays.

"When you received the gameplan on Wednesday morning, you always knew you had a great chance to win if you executed properly," said guard Russ Grimm, who played all 11 of his Redskins seasons for Gibbs before becoming an assistant coach in 1992.

And even if their execution was erratic, the Redskins never thought they were out of a game at halftime.

"No coach could adjust better as a game was going on than Joe Gibbs," said linebacker Matt Millen, who starred for Oakland and San Francisco before playing his final season for Gibbs in 1991.

Gibbs' work ethic resonated with his players.

"Coach Gibbs' players were dedicated because we saw it in him," said defensive end Charles Mann, one of nine Redskins to play a decade or longer for Gibbs. " . . . When I see that bed in his office, how can I cut corners? How I can not spend extra time watching film?"

As safety Brad Edwards put it, "Joe Gibbs is the only coach I have played for who made you feel that he would go to the wall for you. And because he made you feel that way, he got the same out of you."

Edwards will never forget the pep talk he received from Gibbs during his first year in Washington when he was struggling in a reserve role.

"Coach told me that I wasn't playing the way he expected and he knew I could do better," Edwards said. "That conversation changed my career. I still use it as an example of leadership at its finest. He never threatened me. He let me know where I stood. He let me know what he expected and he let me know he was on my side."

Edwards became a starter the next year and intercepted two passes in Washington's Super Bowl XXVI victory over Buffalo, but Gibbs had the same effect on players who were immediate stars.

"Joe was more than a boss," said cornerback Darrell Green, a 10-year starter for Gibbs. "He was a friend. Joe and I talked about marriage before I got married.

Coach.

Years: 1981-92.

Stats: 140-65, three Super Bowl titles, eight playoff berths.

Greatest season: The Redskins went 17-2, won by an average of 16.3 points and won the Super Bowl in 1991.

Honors: Coach of the Year, 1982-83; Hall of Fame, 1996.

Today: Owner NASCAR team, NFL analyst for NBC.

Joe explained to me about postpartum syndrome when my wife had our first child. I was able to cry in front of him when my grandfather passed away. I can tell my children that if they work for someone like Joe they'll be blessed."

Said tight end James Jenkins, who was born-again as a rookie with help from active Christian Gibbs, "Getting to know Joe Gibbs and his staff changed my life. I was kind of going through life taking things for granted, without any real responsibilities or concerns. Joe made me see the opportunities I had before me and showed me I should be thankful for them."

However, the three nights a week Gibbs slept on a bed in his Redskin Park office came at a price to his health and family life and ultimately led to his stunning 1993 retirement. Gibbs came home late one night and leaned down to kiss his sleeping son only to be shocked to discover that his baby boy had sprouted facial hair.

Gibbs, on the brink of exhaustion, wanted to see younger son Coy play for Stanford, having missed elder son J.D.'s career at William & Mary. And the driven coach admitted he had lost some of the superhuman drive with nothing more for him to prove with the Redskins.

"What else was I going to do in coaching really?" Gibbs said. "Go to the Super Bowl again? There comes a certain point where, what are the challenges?"

Gibbs did consider coaching the expansion Carolina Panthers in 1995 but opted to stay in the stock car pits and in the NBC studio as an NFL analyst. Not that Gibbs doesn't miss the good times in Washington. Gibbs, his players and his assistants, six of whom worked for him during his entire career with the Redskins, were his second family.

"The thing that I will miss the most is the relationship that I have with my assistant coaches and the play-ers," Gibbs said during his retirement speech. "The thing I've always loved about sports is trying to put something together, to get a group of guys to do something that requires sacrifice and hard work. . . . We had great teams because of the people we've had."

Gibbs said his Hall of Fame election wasn't so much about his success as it was "a celebration of an era . . . a heck of an era."

It was an era in which the Redskins went to the Super Bowl via: defense and timely kicking by Mark Moseley (1982); a record-setting, opportunistic defense and the highest-scoring team in NFL history led by quarterback Joe Theismann (1983); two quarterbacks, Jay Schroeder and Doug Williams, and replacement players (1987); and the most dominant team Washington has ever had (1991).

Also, no other NFL coach won Super Bowls in strike seasons or with three quarterbacks: Theismann, Williams and Mark Rypien. Gibbs also reached an NFC Championship Game with Schroeder. None of these passers came close to equaling those achievements under any other coach.

Receiver Art Monk and Green are sure Hall of Famers and Grimm and offensive tackle Joe Jacoby may be enshrined someday, but Gibbs' players readily admit that such rivals as San Francisco, Dallas and Chicago were usually more talented. But they didn't have Washington's spirit.

"Every guy on our teams had character and heart," said linebacker Monte Coleman, a Redskin throughout Gibbs' tenure. "I always remember what [Hall of Fame Dallas coach] Tom Landry said about us. He said, 'The Redskins don't have the most talent, but they know how to play well together.' "

Thanks in large part to their remarkable coach.

photo courtesy of the Washington Redskins

Joe Gibbs maps out strategy for another Redskins victory.

COACH JOE GIBBS

MARK MOSELEY BEATS A RECORD AND THE GIANTS WITH THIS CLUTCH KICK.

Pressure Kicker

Redskins 15, Giants 14

In the season the Redskins won their first Super Bowl, running back John Riggins earned most of the glory for his dramatic title-winning jaunt. But if not for a man who almost didn't make the team, Riggins and Co. wouldn't have had the opportunity to bask in the spotlight.

The Redskins, who had won eight of their final 11 games in 1981 after an 0-5 start under rookie coach Joe Gibbs, headed to training camp in 1982 confident they were playoff-bound. Veterans such as quarterback Joe Theismann, running backs Riggins and Joe Washington and safeties Mark Murphy and Curtis Jordan were meshing nicely with such youngsters as receivers Art Monk and Charlie Brown, offensive linemen Joe Jacoby and Russ Grimm and defensive end Dexter Manley.

One of the biggest questions was at kicker where longtime stalwart Mark Moseley had fought back from an atrocious start in 1980 only to endure another so-so year in 1981. The coaches had brought rookie Dan Miller to Carlisle to give Moseley his stiffest competition in memory.

"I had a bad year [just 5-of-13 on field goals beyond 40 yards] the year before because I kept pulling a muscle," Moseley said. "Joe Gibbs and his staff didn't have much allegiance to me because it was their first year. I knew they would bring someone to camp to challenge me. But put a challenge in front of me and I'll go after it hard."

Moseley did. Still, special teams coach Wayne Sevier acknowledged, "There was a point where I thought Dan was ahead."

In fact, before the final preseason game at Cincinnati, Gibbs told Moseley that Miller was going to do all the kicking. Moseley was mentioned in trade rumors as the 0-3 Redskins searched for a defensive lineman to shore up their pass rush.

"I'm not getting the opportunity to determine my own fate," Moseley said at the time. "I have the utmost confidence that the coaches will make the right decision. I'm not criticizing them. [But] I'm not so sure that

the decision will be based on what I'm capable of doing rather [than on] what Danny can do."

Years later, Moseley still remembers feeling "totally helpless." However, Miller missed both of his field-goal attempts as the Redskins concluded a winless preseason with a 28-21 loss. The rookie was put on injured reserve. Moseley was starting a ninth Washington season. It was one neither he nor the Redskins would ever forget.

The season began in Philadelphia. Theismann coolly brought his team back from deficits of 10-0 and 27-14, but with a minute left, 6-foot-9 Harold Carmichael grabbed a lob from Ron Jaworski in the end zone to put the Eagles back on top, 34-31. Theismann drove the Redskins to the Philadelphia 31 and Moseley came on to pound the overtime-forcing 48-yard field goal through the uprights. Washington won the coin toss. Two big catches by Monk set up Moseley for the game-winning 26-yarder.

Riggins and Jordan nearly drowned in the end zone during the monsoon which enveloped Tampa Stadium during the following week's 21-13 victory. And then came the strike. It lasted 57 days, more than twice as long as anyone figured. Some teams' players went on vacation, but not Washington's. Although Gibbs said he felt "helpless . . . caught in the middle" between the

<table>
<tr><td colspan="6">REDSKINS 15, GIANTS 14</td></tr>
<tr><td></td><td>1</td><td>2</td><td>3</td><td>4</td><td>Total</td></tr>
<tr><td>Giants</td><td>7</td><td>7</td><td>0</td><td>0</td><td>14</td></tr>
<tr><td>Redskins</td><td>0</td><td>3</td><td>6</td><td>6</td><td>15</td></tr>
</table>

FIRST QUARTER
NY - Perkins 28 pass from Brunner (Danelo kick), NY 7-0

SECOND QUARTER
W - Moseley FG 20, NY 7-3
NY - Woolfolk 1 run (Danelo kick), NY 14-3

THIRD QUARTER
W - Washington 22 run (kick failed), NY 14-9

FOURTH QUARTER
W - Moseley 31 FG, NY 14-12
W - Moseley 42 FG, W 15-14

warring players and owners, his striking players stuck by him.

"Just before the strike took place, coach Gibbs called a few of us in," Monk recalled. "He really stressed the importance of the players getting together and practicing even though we were going to be on strike. He said, 'Whatever else happens, I want you guys to stay together.' We did. We practiced five days a week. We had meetings. I don't think we anticipated the strike would last as long as it did. It seemed like it wasn't ever going to end. [But] that's what really kept us together when we came back."

When the Redskins returned, it was as if the season hadn't even been interrupted. They beat the Giants 27-17 in New York and edged the Eagles 13-9 thanks to field goals of 43 and 45 yards by Moseley - running his streak to 13 in a row over two seasons. Dallas then whipped Washington 24-10, but the Redskins rebounded behind Moseley's four field goals to win 12-7 at St. Louis.

Washington was 5-1 atop the NFC East and - in the abbreviated nine-game season - just one victory shy of its first playoff berth in six years. But next up was the Dec. 19 rematch with New York at RFK. It would be a cold, wet afternoon, hardly ideal kicking conditions.

"It was a miserable day," Jacoby said. "We always had tough battles with the Giants and this was another slugfest. Another classic at RFK."

And the Redskins had their square-toed not-so-secret weapon.

"The Giants hated to play us because of Moseley," said offensive tackle George Starke, remembering the kicker's overtime game-winner in 1981 at Giants Stadium. "They knew when it came down to it, we had a three-point advantage."

But the way the Redskins played in the first half, Moseley didn't seem likely to be much of a factor. The Giants, still thinking playoffs themselves at 3-3 and eager to avenge their loss in the Meadowlands, were extremely opportunistic.

Washington took the opening kickoff and marched to the New York 34, but Theismann's pass for Brown was intercepted by linebacker Brian Kelley. Five plays later, quarterback Scott Brunner passed 28 yards to receiver Johnny Perkins for a 7-0 Giants lead. The Redskins drove again, but this time Monk fumbled away a 25-yard gain when hit by cornerback Terry Jackson. Safety Beasley Reece recovered at the New York 10.

The Giants didn't force a turnover on the Redskins' next possession, but they did prevent them from converting a first-and-goal situation into a touchdown. Moseley's 20-yard field goal put Washington on the scoreboard as the second quarter began.

Midway through the period, Kelley picked off Theismann again, this time at the Washington 48. New York did nothing with this break, but got another when middle linebacker Harry Carson tipped Theismann's throw into Jackson's hands at the Washington 39. Five plays later, halfback Butch Woolfolk scored from a yard out with 18 seconds left in the half. The Giants, outgained 193-97, led 14-3.

"I told them [the players] we were fortunate not to be further behind," Gibbs said. "I told them if we could put together a sustained drive and score a touchdown, we'd be right back in the game."

The Redskins followed their coach's orders after stopping the Giants' opening possession of the second half. Riggins and Washington did most of the early damage and then Theismann finally got on track, connecting with tight end Don Warren for 17 yards and Brown for 24.

On first-and-10 from the New York 22, Washington was supposed to run right and throw an option pass to Monk. But the Giants had the play figured out so Washington dashed back to the left. The only teammate on that side was Theismann.

"I saw one friendly jersey and it was Joe," Washington said. "I had to get by one Giant [Jackson] or flip the ball to Joe like a wishbone quarterback."

Theismann made like a Hog and took Jackson down with a diving body block which sprung Washington for the touchdown that narrowed the gap to 14-9. It stayed that way as Moseley, incredibly, missed the extra point when the wet ball slipped off his foot.

Neither offense did anything for the rest of the quarter, but as the final period began and the snow began falling more rapidly, Gibbs went to the "Riggo Drill." The 230-pound runner carried on eight of 10 plays, setting up Moseley's 31-yard field goal which tied Garo Yepremian's NFL record of 20 straight. Washington trailed 14-12 with 6:23 remaining.

Gibbs gambled when the Redskins got the ball back and it looked foolish when Kelley stopped Riggins on fourth-and-1 from the Washington 40. However, linebackers Mel Kaufman (solo), Neal Olkewicz and Larry Kubin (shared) responded with consecutive sacks of

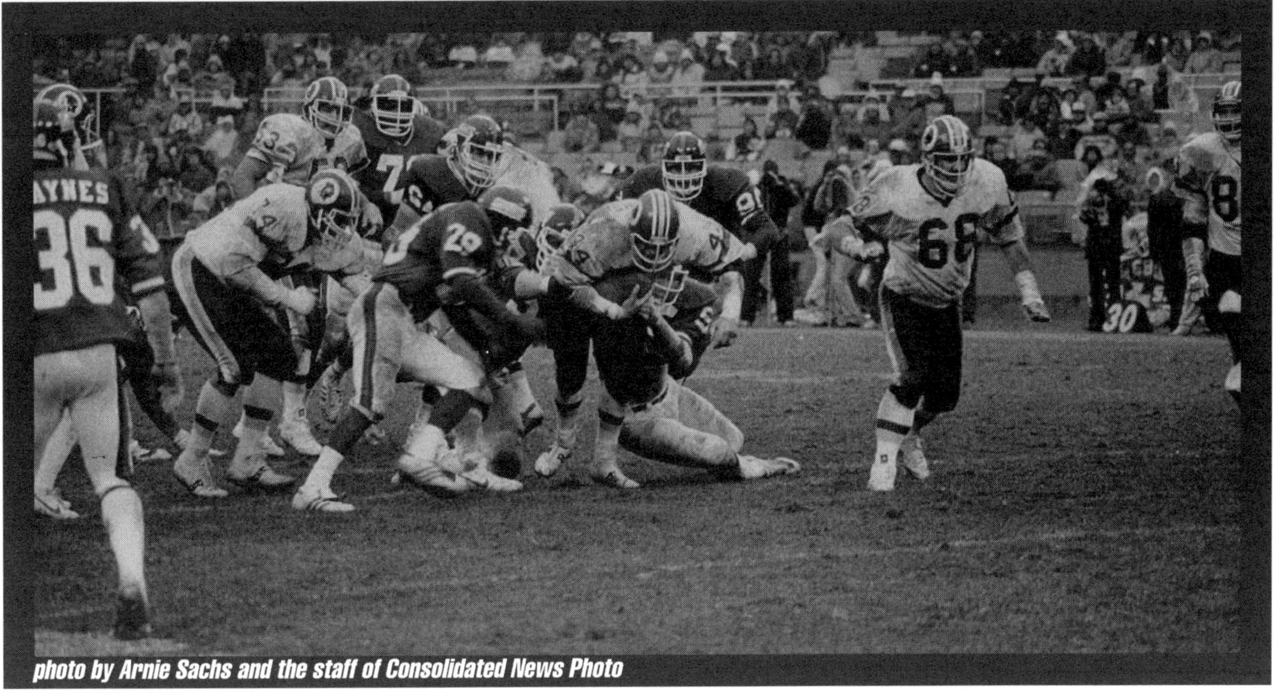

John Riggins muscles for extra yardage against the Giants.

Brunner and the Redskins took over at their 29 with 3:38 to play.

Tight end Doc Walker got open for a 20-yard gain to put the ball in New York territory. Then on a critical third-and-5 from the 39, Theismann found Brown between two Giants for 14 yards.

"When a kicker is on a roll like that . . . you're confident that when you get on the other side of the 30, you've got three points," Jacoby said.

Theismann said no kicker was better than Moseley in bad weather or in the clutch. And this situation had plenty of each of those elements.

The Giants felt the same way. According to Moseley, New York's former all-Pro linebacker Lawrence Taylor has told him, "We knew on that last drive we couldn't let Washington into field-goal range or we were dead."

But back then Moseley was just trying to keep his right foot dry on the sideline with a down-lined slipper and a plastic garbage bag which his wife Sharon had passed down from the stands.

"Cold weather is tough on a kicker," said Moseley. "The ball gets real hard and you've got to hit it just right to make it go straight. Your feet get cold and you don't get that feeling you need to have, like when you're playing good golf and you just know you're going to make the shot. But that's the way I felt when I was kick-

ing. My mind would convince me that I was going to make the kick.

"I never worried about the distance," Moseley continued. "I was so confident, it could have been from 60 yards out. It was almost like destiny. I had been seeing myself setting the record and winning the game all week. I even had a dream about it."

But this was no dream. After three runs by Riggins and a holding penalty on Walker, it was Moseley time. There were 11 seconds left. Gibbs knelt in prayer. The field goal would be from 42 yards out. For a victory, a playoff spot and a record. Moseley trotted onto the field. All he said was his usual, "Let's get it, Joe," to long-time holder Theismann.

Big Dave Butz stomped out a smooth spot for Theismann. The snow was falling so hard Moseley could barely see the goalposts, but Jeff Bostic's snap and Theismann's hold were perfect. And despite being grazed by the hand of New York's Byron Hunt, so was the kick. The Redskins won, 15-14.

"It was like a Hollywood script; you couldn't have written it any better," Murphy said in the raucous locker room.

"I hit that ball so well, it never even moved when that guy got his hand on it," Moseley said. "It was the most exciting moment in my life other than getting married and having my children."

MARK MOSELEY

Mark Moseley

If not for one coach's bad dream, another's good memory and his own refusal to believe he didn't belong, kicker Mark Moseley might have been one of those forgotten NFL players – a guy who lasted a couple of seasons and was never heard from again.

Moseley, a 14th-round draft choice, surprisingly beat out veteran Sam Baker in 1970 in Philadelphia. But the Eagles kept rookie Happy Feller over Moseley the next summer. Moseley went to Houston and led the AFC in field-goal percentage. After the Oilers lost their 1972 opener to Denver, rookie coach Bill Peterson approached Moseley in the parking lot outside the club's headquarters.

"He said he had a dream that Dan Pastorini, who was our punter as well as our quarterback, had been injured," Moseley recalled, still incredulous 24 years later. "I had just kicked two field goals against Denver. Peterson told me he needed a kicker who could also punt and I had been cut."

Pastorini didn't get hurt. New kicker Skip Butler did last five seasons, but Peterson was fired in 1973 with a 1-18 record.

A stunned Moseley almost caught on with Cleveland, but wound up going back to school, digging septic tanks and leasing real estate in his native Texas. His wife, Sharon, would hold the ball as he kicked field goals every day after work. But Moseley didn't just kick. He ran with a leather vest whose pockets he weighed down with sand. He lifted weights to add 20 pounds of strength. However, the 1973 season came and went and no club called.

"Never give up on yourself," Moseley said at the 1987 press conference to announce his retirement. "If you conclude that you can play the game, don't take anyone's word that you can't. Keep plugging away. Set your goal and work toward it. And I mean work. Every day. If your assessment was correct, you will succeed."

That formula of hard work plus faith equals success was seared into Moseley's core on Feb. 7, 1974, when his phone rang at 7:30 a.m.

"It was [coach] George Allen calling to ask if I wanted to play for the Redskins," Moseley said. "I had kicked a couple of field goals in a monsoon at RFK in 1971. There were probably six inches of water on the field. George remembered that and he had [Redskins photographer] Nate Fine find out who that kicker from the Oilers had been."

Moseley made seven straight field goals in the preseason of 1974 and when he beat Cleveland with a last-second 43-yarder, incumbent Curt Knight was cut and the job was Moseley's. He kept it until October 1986 when a tearful coach Joe Gibbs released the 38-year-old veteran.

Along the way, Moseley would become the league's fourth-leading career scorer, set the season record for points by a kicker, connect on a then-record 23 straight field goals and become the only kicker ever to be named the NFL's Most Valuable Player. And Moseley did so with straight-ahead boots when all but one other kicker was using the soccer-style method. But other kickers didn't have his strength or rhythm.

There was another element to Moseley's success: the rare ability to block out the worst distractions and concentrate on the 1.3-second routine of step, plant, kick, follow-through.

In 1979, Moseley's sister was raped and murdered in her home. His wife underwent cancer surgery in 1980. That year he missed 10 of his first 14 field goal tries but made no excuses. Naturally, he hit five field goals in the next game, including two from beyond 50 yards.

"I never let things bother me mentally," said Moseley, proud of his tough Texas roots which included summers lifting 500-pound 'sticks' at his father's pulpwood company. "If I missed a kick, I didn't make excuses. It was my fault."

Said offensive tackle George Starke, "In his own way, Mark was a warrior. He always thought he was a football player. He wasn't just some guy who kicked a ball."

So much so that at age 48, Moseley planned to play a second season for the semi-pro Fredericksburg (Va.) Generals in 1996. He drew his first unsportsmanlike conduct penalty the year before after making the tackle on a kickoff and responding to a forearm to the head with a punch.

"My wife thinks I'm crazy," admitted Moseley. "But I can still hit almost every kick from 45 yards in and I love the game."

As A Redskin

Position: Kicker.

Years: 1974-86.

Stats: Club records of 1,207 points, 263 field goals, 417 extra points. Retired as NFL's fourth-leading scorer.

Greatest season: He hit his first 20 field goal tries as NFL MVP in 1982.

Honors: NFL MVP, 1982; Pro Bowl, 1979, 1982.

Today: Travel agency owner, Northern Virginia.

DAVE BUTZ

Dave Butz

Defensive lineman Dave Butz spent the night before a 1987 game against the New York Jets in Arlington Hospital, hooked to an IV pumping him with 11 quarts of fluids. At 9 a.m. the day of the game, he bolted for RFK Stadium, played the entire way, recorded a game-saving sack and even received a game ball after the 17-16 victory.

Then he spent the night in the hospital. Doctors filled him with six more quarts of fluids. In one week, an intestinal disorder caused him to lose 24 pounds.

"But I never missed a meeting or a practice," Butz said.

Before his lone Pro Bowl appearance, in 1983, Butz was helped to the team bus by Dallas' Randy White. Butz, sick again, carried a plastic bag with him to the stadium. Just in case. The bus stopped at a pharmacy, Butz received some medication, took a shot and then made 2 1/2 sacks in the game.

"I'd spent my career trying to get to the Pro Bowl, and I wasn't going to let some sickness stop it," said Butz, who lasted longer than most defensive linemen. "I kept throwing up, going to the bathroom all the time. But I wasn't going to let that keep me from playing."

Nothing kept Butz from playing in the 1980s. Actually, one thing did. The only game he missed from 1980-88 came in 1984 when food poisoning sidelined him. Other than that, No. 65 was a staple in the Redskins' lineup. He played until he was 38 and was the second oldest player in the league when he retired.

"You could count on Dave," said guard Russ Grimm.

In a Sept. 14, 1986, game against the Raiders, Butz broke his left thumb and missed seven plays. But he returned after halftime — despite protests from his wife Candyce — with a cast and finished the game. And season. Doctors drilled two 3 1/2-inch pins that went through the thumb to the bone, holding his thumb in place.

"That's extremely painful," Butz said. "There was no pad that would protect that. When I got hit in the pins and the pins were in the bone, it didn't feel good."

The Redskins obtained Butz via free agency in 1975, but they had to give St. Louis two No. 1 draft picks and a No. 2 in compensation for losing the 1973 all-rookie performer. Butz missed the 1974 season after ripping up his knee in the season opener and requiring reconstructive surgery.

Some Redskins doubted he would become Mr. Reliable after he missed six games in 1977 with an ankle sprain.

"I believe Dave was taught how to play through pain [from the veteran Redskins]," said cornerback Pat Fischer. "He developed into a great courageous football player. I don't believe anyone would have guessed that from the first year or two he was there."

Nor could anyone foresee Butz's importance in the Redskins' lineup. His role: plug the middle of the line by occupying two blockers. That was something the 6-foot-7, Butz, then one of the few 300-pounders in the NFL, did well. This was a man with a solid work ethic who took pride in doing his job. Even if it meant sacrificing himself.

But some of his teammates, while acknowledging his value, also wondered if Butz was an underachiever. They saw a monster of a man who only occasionally dominate the guy in front of him. Others, however, saw Butz's importance in the details of his work. Those are the ones who fed off him.

"Because Dave was so big, people expected more," said linebacker Mel Kaufman. "To me, he did what he was asked to do. He made [defensive tackle] Darryl Grant a better player. He made defensive end Charles Mann better and he made me better. [Butz] had two people blocking him. That helps out everybody."

John Gesek, who played against Butz as a rookie guard with the Los Angeles Raiders in 1987, said, "It was like blocking a house. I couldn't even think about moving him."

Did Butz always enjoy the role of smacking into two guys on every play? No. But his answer reveals the attitude that helped him survive.

"It was my job," said Butz, who worked on a construction crew loading concrete before being drafted. "I didn't have to enjoy it. I was bullheaded and stubborn. That's a great combination, but the only thing it is good for is football. You're definitely a fool. But when they sing, 'I did it my way,' boy that's the truth. I did it my way."

As A Redskin

Position: Defensive tackle.

Years: 1975-88.

Stats: Third-best in club history in sacks (59.5) and games played (203).

Greatest season: Led team with 11 1/2 sacks, forced team-high five fumbles, recovered one and made 69 tackles in 1983.

Honors: Pro Bowl, 1983, all-Pro 1983.

Today: Part-owner and manager of The Orchards Golf Course, Belleville, Ill.

DARRYL GRANT PROVES AN UNLIKELY HERO IN THE NFC CHAMPIONSHIP GAME.

Doomsday for Dallas

Redskins 31, Cowboys 17

As the Washington Redskins geared up for the strike-elongated 1982 postseason, few of them understood what they were getting into. Only nine had been in an NFL playoff game. Just six players remained from Washington's last playoff team six years before: quarterback Joe Theismann, running back John Riggins, kicker Mark Moseley, offensive tackle George Starke, defensive tackle Dave Butz and cornerback Joe Lavender. None played in the Redskins postseason victory.

More than half the players - 28 - were in their first, second or third NFL season and Joe Gibbs was only in his second year as a head coach.

"I had no idea things would turn out the way they did that year," said Art Monk, then a third-year receiver. "We were still trying to learn coach Gibbs' offensive system. We were a young, rebuilding team. We had a couple of stars here and there, but overall, we weren't that talented. But there was a sense of closeness. We played well together. Everyone played with a sense of dedication."

Linebacker Monte Coleman, an 11th-round pick in 1979, noted, "We probably had more [undrafted players] than draft choices. Coach Gibbs knew what to look for in a player, the guys who could fit into his system. And they didn't have to be the high picks."

Indeed, such starters as offensive tackle Joe Jacoby, center Jeff Bostic, tight end Doc Walker, linebackers Mel Kaufman and Neal Olkewicz and safety Mark Murphy hadn't been drafted. Starke, receiver Charlie Brown and linebacker Rich Milot had seen more than 180 players chosen before their names were called.

"Some of us were happy just to be playing in the NFL," Kaufman said.

During his induction speech to the Hall of Fame in 1996, Gibbs said he often surprises people by naming special-teamers as Pete Cronan and Otis Wonsley as his greatest players.

"They were guys that gave their guts, covered those kickoffs and made all the rest of us look good," Gibbs said in admiration.

But the no-name Redskins, who had rebounded from an 0-5 start in 1981 to win eight of their final 11 games, would establish themselves in 1982. They won their two games before the eight-week players' strike and their first two afterwards. The next week, Dallas intercepted Theismann three times and sacked him seven times at RFK to ruin Washington's perfect season with a 24-10 rout, but the Redskins squeaked by St. Louis and the New York Giants to clinch a playoff spot.

Washington had been eking out victories with defense and Moseley's record-setting leg. But as postseason neared, the offense caught fire in 27-10 and 28-0 poundings of New Orleans and St. Louis, respectively. Top receiver Monk was lost for the season when he broke a toe against the Cardinals, but the Redskins still headed into the playoffs on a roll.

"When our offense started to click, we were unstoppable," Moseley said. "We had an aura about us. Coach Gibbs had convinced us we were good. He gave us so much confidence it was phenomenal."

As the NFC's best team at 8-1, Washington had home field advantage throughout the conference playoffs and that would prove a huge factor.

Detroit was the first postseason visitor to RFK in

REDSKINS 31, COWBOYS 17					
	1	2	3	4	Total
Cowboys	3	0	14	0	17
Redskins	7	7	7	10	31

FIRST QUARTER
D - Septien 27 FG, D 3-0
W - Brown 19 pass from Theismann (Moseley kick), W 7-3

SECOND QUARTER
W - Riggins 1 run (Moseley kick), W 14-3

THIRD QUARTER
D - Pearson 6 pass from Hogeboom (Septien kick), W 14-10
W - Riggins 4 run (Moseley kick), W 21-10
D - Johnson 23 pass from Hogeboom (Septien kick), W 21-17

FOURTH QUARTER
W - Moseley 29 FG, W 24-17
W - Grant 10 interception return (Moseley kick), W 31-17

10 years. Five-foot-7 Alvin Garrett, who had six career catches and was only playing because Monk and backup Virgil Seay were hurt, grabbed three touchdown passes from Theismann. Cornerback Jeris White returned an interception 77 yards for a score. Riggins, who had been resting a sore thigh the previous two weeks, rushed for 119 yards.

The Redskins romped 31-7 as "The Fun Bunch" of Garrett, Walker, Seay, Wonsley, Don Warren, Charlie Brown and Clarence Harmon began its routine of collective high-fives to celebrate Washington touchdowns.

Next up was Minnesota. By halftime the final score of 21-7 was set thanks to Washington drives of 66, 70 and 71 yards. Garrett keyed one march with a 46-yard catch off a flea flicker and scored the third touchdown after the Vikings had closed within 14-7. The defense, which held on its own 15, 28 and 39 in the second half, had now allowed just two touchdowns in 14 quarters.

"It was the kind of game we didn't want to get into," said Vikings coach Bud Grant. "We got 14 points behind and let them run the ball."

Riggins, 33, carried a remarkable 37 times for a career-high 185 yards before taking off his helmet and bowing to the crowd.

"They said John was washed up three years ago," Milot marveled.

"Riggins just came blowing by us all day," lamented Minnesota linebacker Scott Studwell. "We were getting beaten at the line of scrimmage and we just couldn't fill the right holes."

Finally, it was Dallas time.

"When we were beating Detroit in the fourth quarter, the fans started cheering 'We want Dallas,' " recalled Charley Casserly, then the Redskins' assistant general manager. "Then we play Minnesota. As soon as we make it 7-0, the chant starts again. 'We Want Dallas.' It's the first quarter! And that continued through-out the game."

The fans weren't the only ones who wanted Dallas.

"My rookie season [1979], we went to Dallas for the final game with a chance to clinch a playoff spot," Coleman said. "We win and we're in. We're kicking their butts, but they came from behind to beat us 35-34. That was the first time I ever cried after a game. The Cowboys were so arrogant. I hated them because of their arrogance."

Kaufman said the Cowboys, who hadn't missed the playoffs since 1974, didn't respect the Redskins. They weren't the only ones.

The strike had eliminated the week off between the championship games and the Super Bowl and word had spread that the vendors in California had imported Dallas, not Washington, merchandise. Also, the Cowboys were planning to fly directly to Pasadena from D.C. Neither of those news items sat well with the men in burgundy and gold. Or their fans.

"There were more people in the stadium an hour before the game than I've ever seen and since it was a 12:30 start, they were there at 11:30 in the morning," Casserly recalled. "As Dallas was walking out for warmups, the chant started again: 'We Want Dallas. We Want Dallas.' When we came out for the introductions, it was deafening."

And the stands were shaking up and down.

"The thing I remember the most was the stands," Coleman said. "They were rocking and rolling. Before the game people were screaming, 'We Want Dallas. We Want Dallas.' A cold chill just kind of crept over me. I've never had it since. It was unreal."

Said Moseley, "I don't think Dallas ever had a chance."

The emotions were so high that Boss Hog, offensive line coach Joe Bugel, uptight about how his young line would fare against the Cowboys' Randy White, Too Tall Jones and Co. was puffing cigarettes even though he didn't even smoke. After the national anthem ended, Bugel spotted Dallas defensive line coach Ernie Stautner across the field and gave him an obscene gesture.

Walker's only concern was that all that emotion would be wasted before the game, and indeed it was Dallas which drove 75 yards to start things off. But the defense held the Cowboys at the 10 and they had to settle for a 27-yard field goal by Rafael Septien.

Theismann led Washington right back down the field. The drive reached the Dallas 19 when the quarterback called an X-post pattern for Brown. Moments later, the receiver was in the end zone with the ball.

"Charlie felt there was no human being anywhere who could cover him," Walker said. "And he would tell Joe in the huddle."

Dallas did stop Washington's next march because Moseley missed a 27-yard field goal try, but not long afterwards, Tony Peters forced Rod Hill to fumble Jeff Hayes' punt. Coleman recovered at the Dallas 11. Four plays later, Riggins was in the end zone for a 14-3 lead.

Things looked even rosier for the Redskins when defensive end Dexter Manley leveled Cowboys quarterback Danny White with 32 seconds left in the half. White walked off, but his concussion would keep him on the bench the rest of the day. Gary Hogeboom, who had thrown just eight career passes, replaced White.

Washington got another break when Mike Nelms fumbled the second-half kickoff only to have teammate Nick Giaquinto recover. However, Hayes' short punt gave the Cowboys the ball at the Washington 38 and Hogeboom needed just six plays to hit receiver Drew Pearson for a touchdown. Nelms redeemed himself with a 76-yard kickoff return, setting up a 4-yard score by Riggins, but Hogeboom engineered a 14-play, 84-yard march capped off by his 23-yard touchdown pass to Butch Johnson. With 3:25 left in the *third* quarter, the lead had shrunk to 21-17.

"We were getting real nervous," Kaufman said.

Hogeboom drove Dallas to the Washington 23 as the fourth quarter began, but Septien missed from the 42. Jones stopped Riggins for no gain on third-and-1 when the Redskins got the ball back and after the punt, Dallas took over at its 32.

Kaufman and White had practiced a scheme where the cornerback would line up inside of the linebacker when they figured the Cowboys would try a certain pattern.

"Jeris and I talked about it in the huddle right before that first down play and it happened just the way we figured," Kaufman said. "Hogeboom was going for receiver Tony Hill and I don't think he even saw me."

Kaufman's interception set up a 29-yard Moseley field goal which widened the lead to 24-17, but there was still 7:12 to go. On first down, the Redskins sensed Hogeboom was going back to a screen to all-Pro halfback Tony Dorsett which had gained 25 yards earlier.

"My first read was pass rush," said defensive tackle Darryl Grant, who had been drafted on the ninth round out of Rice as a guard the year before. "But when I decided it was a screen, I stopped and headed to where I thought it was going to be."

Grant thought correctly. Manley leapt in Hogeboom's face and tipped the ball up in the air. It landed right in the hands of Grant, who high-stepped 10 yards to the end zone as the fans went wild.

The touchdown finally took the life out of the Cowboys. And then the Redskins went to the "Riggo Drill."

"We ran 50-Gut [Riggins up the middle] nine times in a row," Bostic said. "On the third or fourth one, I told Russ let's have some fun. We're the young kids on the block. We're the nobodies. The Cowboys walked the field as if their feet didn't touch the ground. They were America's Team and all that. We came to the line and told Randy, 'We're running the ball at you.' He didn't say anything."

Bostic kept yapping, but White stayed silent. What could he say?

Gibbs was carried off the field after the 31-17 triumph in a scene reminiscent of Allen's victory ride a decade earlier.

"We beat the Cowboys, we're going to the Super Bowl, what else could you want?" said Theismann, who cried with joy as the fans made the ground shake beneath his feet in the final seconds.

"It's their year," Pearson said. "They made the plays to make it happen. It's the year of the Redskin."

Pearson knew what he was talking about. The following Sunday, Riggins broke away from Don McNeal's tackle and rumbled 43 yards into history as the Redskins rallied to beat Miami 27-17 and win Super Bowl XVII.

JOHN RIGGINS

John Riggins

One of Joe Gibbs' first priorities as the new Redskins coach in 1981 was ending John Riggins' one-year holdout. Gibbs traveled to Riggins' farm in Lawrence, Kan., for a morning meeting only to find his potential star running back wearing combat fatigues and drinking beer.

"You need to get me back there," Riggins told Gibbs. "I'll make you famous."

Gibbs figured Riggins for a "fruitcake" and "egomaniac." No matter, Gibbs could always trade Riggins after he returned. But two days after the meeting, Riggins told Gibbs he would agree to return given one proviso in his contract — a no-trade clause.

Riggins played five more seasons and fulfilled his pledge to Gibbs. The Redskins won Super Bowl XVII over the Miami Dolphins 27-17, Riggins led the postseason charge by rushing for 100 yards in a record four straight playoff games. The following year, Riggins set a Redskins rushing record with 1,347 yards and an NFL mark of 24 touchdowns. Washington got back to the Super Bowl, but lost to the Los Angeles Raiders, 38-9.

Known as "Riggo," "Mr. January" and "The Diesel," Riggins was as flamboyant off the field as he was flashy on it. He loved being football's version of James Dean, even sporting a Mohawk haircut because "I always wanted one as a kid, but my parents wouldn't let me. I did it to show I was my own boss. Ah, really, I just did it for the fun of it."

Riggins liked being a free spirit even if it meant upsetting others. He once told Supreme Court Justice Sandra Day O'Connor to "Loosen up, Sandy baby" at a black-tie affair before falling asleep on the floor during Vice President George Bush's speech. Riggins practiced in work boots, once painted his toenails green and took a bow at midfield during the 1983 playoff game against Minnesota.

"Contrary to popular opinion, I'm not a flake," Riggins said in 1983. "Maybe I've taken a game that is respected by so many sportswriters and just played with it, and they don't like it."

But many loved Riggins' unconventional lifestyle.

"Characters make up a football team," said Sam Huff, a Hall of Fame linebacker who broadcast many of Riggins' games. "They don't read the Bible or become exemplary citizens, but at 1 o'clock John laid it out on the field. Down deep, John Riggins is a hell of a person."

At 6-foot-2, 240 pounds, Riggins was certainly built like a diesel engine, only this one could fly.

"John was very deceiving when he got in the open," said Redskins offensive tackle Joe Jacoby. "A lot of people think someone that big isn't fast."

Shortly before the 1982 playoffs, Riggins felt his hair standing on end and his neck tingling. It was "The Surge." Riggins told Gibbs he wanted the ball. The more the better.

"Listen, trust me," Riggins told Gibbs. "Give me the football, baby."

The Redskins would gain early leads and then use the "Riggo Drill" of pounding opponents with late ball-control drives. Riggins gained 610 yards in the four postseason games, 253 in the fourth quarter. He accounted for 43.3 percent of the Redskins' offense.

"I did the right thing," he said. "I asked for that one little chance we get occasionally. I grabbed the bull by the horns and said, 'Let's roll!' "

Riggins' finest moment was breaking Miami cornerback Don McNeal's tackle for a 43-yard touchdown run to clinch the Redskins' Super Bowl victory over the Dolphins. He gained 166 yards while earning Most Valuable Players honors. Escaping McNeal wasn't surprising. Teammates said few defenders ever tried tackling Riggins head on.

"John was 260 pounds and defensive backs were 180," offensive tackle George Starke said. "They'd lose IQ points every time they made the tackle."

It was that toughness that made Riggins fit in well with his offensive linemen — the Hogs.

"Sometimes we'd say 'Look, we'll block 10 and you run over one,' " Starke said. "He'd say 'Which one?' We'd tell him that one over there and he'd run over him. He was like a guard carrying the ball. He was as goofy and zany as the rest of us."

And proud of it.

THE HOGS: (L TO R) RUSS GRIMM, FRED DEAN, GEORGE STARKE, MARK MAY, DOC WALKER (SEATED), JOE JACOBY, DON WARREN AND JEFF BOSTIC.

The Hogs

When Joe Bugel coached the Phoenix Cardinals, fans spotted him in airports and recognized him as a football coach. It didn't matter which airport he was in, either. People would run up to him and say the same thing.

"Hey," they'd shout. "There's the Hogs' coach!"

"They didn't even know my name," said Bugel, now Oakland's offensive line coach. "But they knew me as the Hogs coach. That's what people recognized first. I loved that. Every place I've been people ask about the Hogs. Even now with the Raiders."

Imagine how many offensive line coaches ever turn heads in airports. But no NFL offensive line gained more fame or attracted more of a following than the Hogs in Washington. Defensive lines had earned nicknames before — the Rams' Fearsome Foursome, Pittsburgh's Steel Curtain and Minnesota's Purple People Eaters. But an offensive line with a flashy moniker? Please.

The Hogs were a bunch of beefy, no-nonsense players who liked to drink beer, smash a few heads on Sunday and open holes large enough for a diesel. Particularly one named John Riggins. Five gained the most attention and formed the core of the Hogs: left tackle Joe Jacoby, left guard Russ Grimm, center Jeff Bostic, right guard Mark May and right tackle George Starke. At an average size of 6-foot-5 and 280 pounds, they were the NFL's biggest line in the early 1980s.

Tight ends Doc Walker and Don Warren joined in the spotlight as their main roles were blocking. They were big. They liked crashing into defenders. Hence, they were Hogs, too. Riggins, who often watched films with the group, later became an honorary member.

It started innocently in 1982. Bugel gathered his interior linemen before one hot and muggy day during training camp in Carlisle, Pa., and, wanting them to run to the blocking sleds, said, "OK, you Hogs, let's get running down here." Bugel had been looking for something to bond this group. The Hogs fit.

"It was just something to get through training camp," Starke said. "It wasn't intended to be anything."

Bugel said, "We were a big chunky group at the time. Especially Russ. It just caught on. Holy smokes, it just mushroomed. The next thing you know, we bought T-shirts with a big Razorback hog on it. Fortunately for that group, the team accepted it. Coach Joe Gibbs made the statement in front of the team that once you establish a nickname, you'd better back it up."

They did. Individually, they were good. Collectively, they were dominant. Of the Redskins' top five rushing seasons, three came between 1983-85 — the height of the Hogs. That stretch included a then-playoff record of 185 yards rushing against Minnesota in 1982. There were four straight 100-yard rushing games in the playoffs that season.

"Everyone knew they didn't want to be behind us in the second half," Starke said. "Because then the infantry was coming out. You knew you had to stop the Hogs."

Eventually, the Hogs spawned new generations of piglets as linemen such as Jim Lachey, Ed Simmons

The Hogs

Position: Offensive linemen.

Years: 1982-93.

Greatest season: Center Jeff Bostic, guard Russ Grimm and tackle Joe Jacoby made the 1983 Pro Bowl. It was the first time three linemen from one team made it to the same Pro Bowl. That season, the Redskins rushed for a club-record 2,625 yards, averaging 4.2 yards per carry.

Honors: Pro Bowls 1983 (Bostic, Grimm, Jacoby), 84-86 (Grimm, Jacoby), 88 (May).

Today: Grimm is the Redskins' tight ends coach; Jacoby owns a Chrysler/Plymouth dealership in Warrenton, Va.; Bostic is a Redskins analyst for WTTG-TV and WJFK radio; May is a sportscaster for TNT, One-on-One Sports and Mutual Radio and owns an autopark in Montross, Va.; Starke owns Head Hog Barbecue in Bethesda, Md., and is a part-time analyst for WJLA-TV.

and Raleigh McKenzie were adopted into the group. But it's the success of the originals, as well as the team, that made the name stick.

Because of them, there was a Hog poster (which included the five linemen, the two tight ends and guard Fred Dean, a Redskin from 1978-82, decked out in tuxedos and tennis shoes), Hog T-shirts, Head Hog beer, a restaurant and Super Hogs Inc. They even made it into local newspaper personality columns.

"After we beat the Dolphins in [Super Bowl XVII], I remember driving through Los Angeles and there were bedsheets out the window of apartments that said, 'Go Hogs,' " said Starke. "They were even caught up in this Hog thing. I remember thinking 'This thing is so strange.' We got back to Washington and it had gone bananas."

May said, "Now we're in the limelight and we're as large as any running back or quarterback. Before, you'd walk into the grocery store and no one noticed you. Now they know your name. Anywhere you went nationally, you were introduced as a Hog."

It's not as if this were an all-star cast when it was first assembled.

Starke (1973-84) was the veteran of the group, having been drafted in 1971. He was traded to Kansas City, waived, then re-signed with Washington and spent the 1972 season on the taxi squad. Within two years, the Columbia product was starting.

Next came Bostic (1980-93), cut by Philadelphia and signed as a free agent. As a long snapper. By the next season, Bostic, who had played at Clemson, was starting. That's when he and Starke were joined by May (1981-89) and Grimm (1981-91), first-and third-round picks, respectively, from Pitt that season.

All that remained was for the biggest one to join them — the 6-foot-7, 300-pound Jacoby (1981-1993). When he first walked into Gibbs' office as a rookie free agent from Louisville, the future Hall of Fame coach sized up Jacoby and figured he was a defensive tackle.

"I was scared and frightened because I didn't know what to expect," Jacoby remembers about that first meeting. "So I didn't want to correct him."

Yet Jacoby, whose mother died during his rookie-year training camp, started 13 games that season.

"Not bad for a defensive lineman," he said.

Veterans Warren and Walker were the bookends in this attack and the core was formed. In 1982-83, the five interior linemen missed a combined one game.

What Bugel liked about the mix was that the players could grow together. May, Bostic, Grimm and Jacoby were young bachelors who hung out frequently. Jacoby and Grimm lived together for two years — in a pizza-box filled apartment that usually had a pot of spaghetti on the stove. "Neither one of us were culinary delights," Jacoby said.

The Hogs used to park themselves in an old red shed at Redskin Park and guzzle a few beers after practice. Other teammates would often join them. What was discussed there, remained there. The 5 o'clock club, started in 1969, became a tradition the Hogs proudly continued — "We didn't really fight it that much," Jacoby joked.

Another tradition was wearing their Hog T-shirts (a hog with Redskins on its butt and Hog above it) on Thursdays. Or else be fined $5.

This closeness led to the key ingredient of great communication on the field, especially on line calls, when they resorted to personal knowledge.

"We used our wives' names, then after a while we used our kids' names," Grimm said. "When our kids got older, that was time for us to retire.

"You felt bad if you missed a block. Not because you didn't make yards as a team, but because you let the guys down beside you. They were counting on you to do your job."

It was up to Bugel, the line coach from 1981-89, to mold this group. With such young players, he wanted to make sure their egos remained deflated. So he tore into them and they developed a love-hate relationship.

But Bugel's players mostly loved him — Bostic called him the "finest teaching coach" he ever had. When Bugel left for the Cardinals in 1989, the remaining four Hogs presented him with a bracelet, which Bugel said he'll be buried with.

"Joe's saying was, 'It's my way or Trailways' and there's a bus leaving every half hour,' " May recalled. "He meant that. He wanted us not only to be big and good athletes, he wanted us to be smart and think on the run.

"If we had good games, we had a tendency to celebrate a lot. Russ celebrated more than most. If we

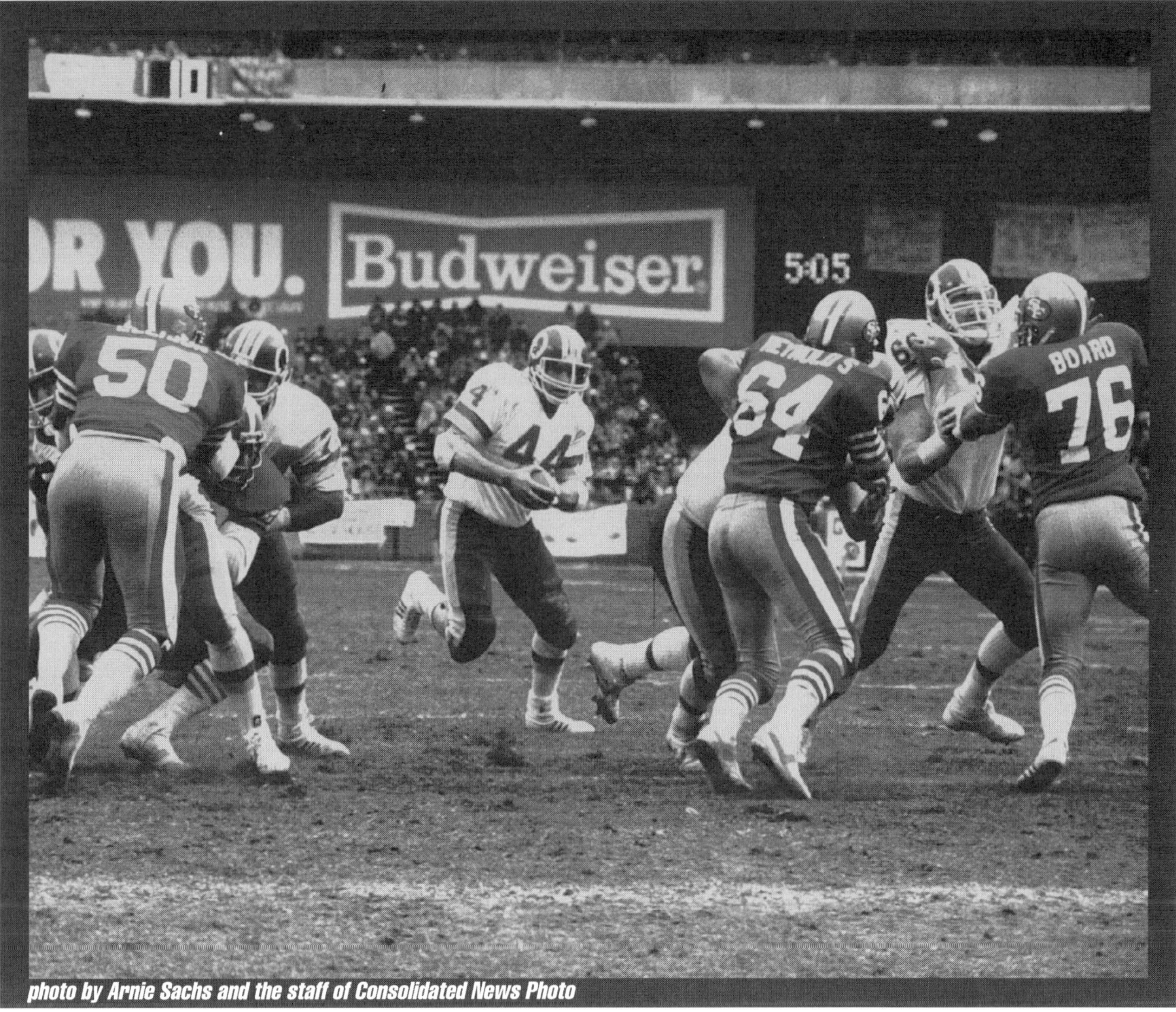

photo by Arnie Sachs and the staff of Consolidated News Photo

The Hogs open up another huge hole for John Riggins.

played badly, Joe would take us out and run the crap out of us on Monday. Sometimes, we played a heck of a game, and would come in watch the film and want to get out of there. He would sense that guys were getting cocky. He would surprise you and take you out and run the crap out of you. There were a lot of days Russ didn't make it. It was a discipline act, but Joe knew that he had to do that to keep us in line."

Bugel said, "I was brutal to them. They even plotted to kill me. I tried to break their spirits when they were young but couldn't do it. [But] the tougher I got on them, the better they played and the more respect they showed."

Two plays made the Hogs famous. Or vice-versa. The gut and the counter trey. The first was straight-ahead smash-mouth football. The second required

pulling action but still resulted in flattened bodies. Sometimes, they'd run the same play nine, 10 times in a row and would tell their opponent — such as Dallas' all-Pro defensive tackle Randy White in the 1982 NFC Championship Game — what was coming. The defenses wilted.

"It was like bludgeoning people with a dull instrument," Bostic said.

They got good at that. And famous. Perhaps Grimm or Jacoby has a shot at the Hall of Fame. Who knows? If none do, that's just as well. After all, this was a group effort.

"If someone said back in 1982 or 1983, did you see Grimm or Bostic play, they'd say, 'Who?'" Bostic said. "But, if they were real football fans and you said, 'Did you see the Hogs?' They'd say, 'Oh, yeah.'"

LITTLE JOE WASHINGTON COMES UP BIG IN THE CLUTCH TO BEAT THE RAIDERS.

The Comeback

Redskins 37, Raiders 35

Joe Gibbs is a humble man. Gibbs may have won three Super Bowls, but there was never any of the genius talk which surrounded Bill Walsh or the legendary label hung on Don Shula. And Gibbs certainly wasn't a cocky blowhard like Buddy Ryan or Jerry Glanville, two coaches who won fewer playoff games in their combined careers than Gibbs did in one season.

Gibbs' Washington teams reflected their coach. They played clean. They didn't talk trash. They shook their opponents' hands afterwards. The Redskins consistently won, but they never carried themselves with the arrogance of the Cowboys.

Except one season. If there was ever a time when Gibbs' Redskins were cocky, it was 1983. They had just won the Super Bowl with a team chock full of 20-somethings. The entire Washington area was in love with them. They were the best and they knew it.

"Coming off that Super Bowl, we *knew* we were good," said linebacker Mel Kaufman, then in his third year.

The Redskins had lost cornerback Jeris White to a contract dispute and safety Tony Peters to a drug suspension but had replaced them with top draft pick Darrell Green and veteran Curtis Jordan. Defensive end Mat Mendenhall had quit, but his spot was taken by his former backup, Todd Liebenstein. However, the rest of the championship lineup was intact. Only quarterback Joe Theismann, running back John Riggins, defensive tackle Dave Butz and offensive tackle George Starke were over 30.

The Redskins had offense - Theismann, Riggins, receiver Charlie Brown and the young line dubbed "The Hogs" - defense - Butz, Green, pass-rushing end Dexter Manley and clever safety Mark Murphy - and special teams - kicker Mark Moseley, return man Mike Nelms and a wild bunch of cover guys led by Greg Williams.

Washington would score 541 points, still an NFL record. Its plus-43 turnover ratio (61 forced, 18 committed) still stands as a record too. Theismann would win the Most Valuable Player award, and he, Brown, Murphy, Butz and Hogs Joe Jacoby, Russ Grimm and Jeff Bostic were Pro Bowl choices.

"We had a no-lose attitude," said linebacker Monte Coleman. "We didn't care how far we were down, we knew we were going to win."

That attitude wasn't even shattered in the season opener on Monday Night Football when Washington blew a 23-3 halftime lead and lost to NFC East nemesis Dallas 31-30.

"I would be angry if we lost because I knew what kind of team we had," said receiver Art Monk. "I would be angry if we didn't play up to our standards."

The Redskins returned to those standards the following three weeks, sandwiching road victories over Philadelphia and Seattle with a home triumph over Kansas City.

Next up was a showdown with the equally talented Los Angeles Raiders of Cliff Branch, Jim Plunkett, Todd Christensen, Lyle Alzado, Howie Long, Ted Hendricks and Lester Hayes, who were only three years removed from their Super Bowl-winning season of 1980. Star

REDSKINS 37, RAIDERS 35					
	1	2	3	4	Total
Raiders	0	7	14	14	35
Redskins	7	10	3	17	37

FIRST QUARTER
W - Riggins 2 run (Moseley kick), W 7-0

SECOND QUARTER
W - Moseley 28 FG, W 10-0
LA - Branch 99 pass from Plunkett (Bahr kick), W 10-7
W - Washington 5 pass from Theismann (Moseley kick), W 17-7

THIRD QUARTER
W - Moseley 29 FG, W 20-7
LA - Muhammad 35 pass from Plunkett (Bahr kick), W 20-14
LA - Muhammad 22 pass from Plunkett (Bahr kick), LA 21-20

FOURTH QUARTER
LA - Christensen 2 pass from Plunkett (Bahr kick), LA 28-20
LA - Pruitt 97 punt return (Bahr kick), LA 35-20
W - Brown 11 pass from Theismann (Moseley kick), LA 35-23
W - Moseley 34 FG, LA 35-30
W - Washington 6 pass from Theismann (Moseley kick), W 37-35

halfback Marcus Allen was hurt, but these were still the big, bad Raiders.

"We thought we were the best team in football," said Raiders linebacker Matt Millen. "We respected the Redskins, but we thought if we could control Riggins, we could win the game. We were really physical and we matched up well with the Redskins."

The Raiders had posted the same 8-1 record as the Redskins in the strike-shortened 1982 season, but while Washington rolled to the Super Bowl title, the Raiders were stunned in the second round of the AFC playoffs by the New York Jets.

"The Raiders had a sense of arrogance like the Cowboys, but they played *football*," Monk said. "They were physical. You knew when you played the Raiders you had a tough ballgame on your hands."

And a dirty one.

"Coach Gibbs said he did not want us fighting with these guys," said Redskins defensive end Charles Mann. "But this is my first chance to justify being a legitimate third-round pick. I saw this game as my opportunity to show these guys I'm just as tough as they are."

The rookie could have made a wiser choice.

"On this special teams play, Otis Wonsley went down and he just decked one of their defensive backs," Mann said. "It was a de-cleater, a play where you hit the guy so hard his cleats go up in the air. I run over and give Otis a high-five and we go jogging off the field. As we do, I look out of the corner of my eye and the DB he decked is coming after Otis. I didn't say anything to Otis, but right before he was about to hit Otis, I turned and just nailed him again.

"Now this guy's a two-time loser. I'm kind of standing over him, telling him, 'You ain't nothing.' But the Raiders' defense is coming on the field and Howie Long comes over unbeknownst to me and smacks me in the back of my head with his forearm and almost knocks me down. I turn around and 'Oh my God, there's Howie Long.' Guys start grabbing me and saying 'Get off the field.' Coach Gibbs is fussing at me, 'What are you doing! I told you not to fight with these guys!' "

Mann was far from alone. Three times the teams were assessed offsetting unsportsmanlike penalties. Starke called it "the toughest game I've ever been in." Long, who called it the "longest, hardest game I've ever played," was in a war with Redskins guard Mark May.

"I would do whatever it took to get the job done," May said. "If it was a leg whip, if I had to hit the guy below the belt, it didn't matter."

Long, who had become friendly with May at the 1981 college scouting combine and would wind up buying cars from him in the 1990s, wasn't happy with his buddy that afternoon.

"If holding was an art, Mark May would be Picasso," Long said. "He hits me after the whistle, but nobody throws a flag. I retaliate and I get penalized. I didn't fly all the way to Washington to get pushed around."

Neither did his teammates after a turnover-plagued start. Jordan's 20-yard interception return to the L.A. 11 set up an early Riggins touchdown. The Redskins failed to take advantage of safety Ken Coffey's interception at the Raiders' 42 or Green's fumble recovery at midfield, but when Kaufman picked off Plunkett's pass for receiver Malcolm Barnwell and raced 23 yards to the L.A. 23, Moseley kicked a 28-yard field goal and it was 10-0 Redskins early in the second quarter.

Plunkett was 1-for-7 and had been sacked twice and intercepted three times, but he was still a smart, resolute veteran. After an exchange of punts left the Raiders on their 1, Plunkett fired long to Branch, who had gotten behind the surprised Washington secondary. Branch would later leave the game with an injury, but the 99-yard touchdown was the longest ever against the Redskins.

Theismann answered with three consecutive first-down throws to Monk, Brown — with a personal foul on Hayes tacked on — and Monk again to move the ball to the L.A. 11. After Riggins carried twice,

Theismann hit halfback Joe Washington for the 5-yard score.

When Manley sacked Plunkett for a 13-yard loss on third-and-seven at the Washington 10 on the next series and Chris Bahr missed a 41-yard field goal try, the Redskins were in command at halftime, 17-7.

Millen said the Raiders didn't feel out of it at halftime, having played their worst and trailing by just 10 points, but Moseley's 29-yarder on Washington's first series of the third quarter seemed mere icing and then Jordan recovered a fumble by Calvin Muhammad.

But when the Raiders got the ball back, Plunkett needed just three plays to reach the end zone on a 25-yard pass to Muhammad. The Redskins went nowhere. This time, it took Plunkett seven plays to hit Muhammad with the 22-yard touchdown. Suddenly, Los Angeles led 21-20.

Theismann found Brown for 33 yards, but Riggins — who had fumbled just once in 1982 — lost the ball on the next play. Cornerback Mike Davis recovered for the Raiders at their 37. Plunkett mixed the run and the pass before spotting Christensen for the 2-yard touchdown toss. Los Angeles had scored three straight touchdowns to take a 28-20 lead.

Washington moved to the Raiders' 47, but after Bostic was caught holding, Jeff Hayes came on to punt. He boomed a 54-yarder to the L.A. 3, but Greg Pruitt danced through Washington's cover team and ran 97 yards to the end zone. In less than 14 minutes, the Raiders had turned a seemingly hopeless 20-7 deficit into a 35-20 advantage.

That's when Joe Washington began to take over. Long had bent Washington's single-bar facemask out of shape earlier in the game, but "Little Joe" wasn't going to be denied.

Overshadowed by Riggins the year before, Washington, the team MVP in 1981, still had some life in his 30-year-old legs. Washington caught a screen from Theismann and zipped up the sideline until Lester Hayes knocked him out on the L.A. 21 after a 67-yard run. Three plays later, Brown caught an 11-yard touchdown from Theismann with 6:15 left.

The Raiders expected an onside kick, but Williams was still able to recover for Washington on the L.A. 32. Theismann found tight end Don Warren for 19 yards but was then dropped for an 18-yard loss by Long, forcing the Redskins to settle for a 34-yard field goal by Moseley which cut the gap to 35-30.

"That day was when I became a big fan of Joe Gibbs," Millen said. "I was calling our defenses and we had taken away his big weapon [Riggins] and Gibbs kept coming up with different options. He gave our coverages fits with the deeper routes to Joe Washington. And Theismann was great. He was totally in control of the offense and he was just going to find a way to beat us."

There was still 4:28 remaining. Coffey dragged Christensen down two yards shy of the first down and the Raiders had to punt. Theismann got the ball back on his 31 with 1:50 to play. Brown, covered by Ted Watts — who had replaced the injured James Davis — ran what he termed "simple ins and outs" to pick up nine, 26 and 28 yards. The Redskins were on the Raiders' 6 with 43 seconds left. After Theismann threw the ball away on first down, Washington circled out of the backfield, eluded linebacker Rod Martin and slid over the middle to make a diving grab of the touchdown pass.

"My job is to get open however I can," Washington said after the game. "I probably could have gone outside, but I saw the middle open and I figured Joe would probably be looking for me in that area. Joe usually sees what I see."

The 55,045 witnesses had seen the teams amass 890 yards of offense in the titanic struggle. Theismann outpassed Plunkett 417 to 372, throwing for an amazing 215 yards in the last 12 minutes alone.

"We had played without Marcus, we had lost Cliff and we still almost beat the champions in their place," Millen said. "We weren't down."

Raiders defensive coordinator Charlie Sumner told Millen he had a feeling the teams would be meeting again . . . in the Super Bowl.

Sumner was right. The Raiders came to Super Bowl XVIII in Tampa four months later with something to prove. The Redskins, whose 48-47 loss at Green Bay had been their only blemish since the opening night one-point loss to Dallas, were looking to party. After all they had already beaten the Raiders and they *were* the champions.

"We were cocky from kicking everybody's behind," Monk said. "We thought the Super Bowl wouldn't be any different."

It was. A healthy Allen ran for 191 yards as the Raiders routed the stunned Redskins 38-9. But not even that crushing defeat could tarnish the luster of one of RFK's most memorable games.

CHARLES MANN

Charles Mann

When Charles Mann arrived in Washington in 1983, he was a 6-foot-6, 235-pound defensive end who wanted nothing more than to show the Redskins were right in choosing him in the third round of the draft.

"Coming from a small school I had a lot to prove," said Mann, who had played at Nevada-Reno. "I felt I had to show I was legitimate."

As a rookie, Mann was so concerned about emulating his teammates that he got in trouble with Torgy Torgeson, his position coach.

"I was very anxious to learn how to be a good football player," said Mann, whose work obligations kept him off the field until his senior year of high school. "I would get done with a pass rush and I would run over to [defensive end] Tony McGee, who had 115 career sacks, and ask him about it. Torgy got a little frustrated. He called my agent who passed the word back to me that I needed to stop listening to Tony and start listening to Torgy to make the team."

Mann didn't play much as a rookie. He spent plenty of time in the weight room with strength coach Dan Riley. "At first I would almost throw up because the work was so intense," said Mann, who weighed 270 pounds when he made his four Pro Bowls. By his second year, Mann was a starter. He remained one for a decade.

"We got lucky with Charles," said Richie Petitbon, who ran the defense during Mann's entire 11-year Redskins career. "He was just a tall skinny kid when we got him, but he could run and he was very intelligent. We felt any time we had something tough mentally, we would put Charles in that spot and he would pick it up like he'd been doing it all along."

Mann's sacks picked up quickly too, rising from three as a rookie to 7 1/2 as a first-year starter to a career-high 14 1/2 in 1985.

"I prided myself on being coachable," Mann said. "That's one of the reasons I was so successful. You could tell me what you wanted done and I could get it done. After three years on the team, I never had to go to another meeting. I went, but I didn't have to. I understood the defense, the philosophy behind it, what they wanted out of me and I could play it well. . . . I had a quickness that Todd Liebenstein, who was in front of me my rookie year, didn't have. Todd was a great technician, but he wasn't going to get any sacks for you whereas I didn't have all the technique yet, but defensive end Dexter [Manley] was bringing pressure and they needed somebody on the opposite side."

Manley talked and smiled even more than the gregarious Mann and was an even better pass-rusher until drugs ruined his career. They racked up 133 sacks during their six years together and rank 1-2 in club history, Manley with 97 1/2 and Mann with 82.

"I remember standing on the sidelines arguing back and forth with Dexter about who was going to get the next sack," Mann said. "It was the hardest competition I've ever been a part of, but I look back at footage of those years with Dexter and I always seemed to have a smile on my face. We were really having fun out there."

Mann's fun lessened when he was regularly double-teamed after Manley left in 1989, but Mann rebounded with 11 1/2 sacks as the Redskins won the Super Bowl in 1991. Knees that had been operated on six times and would require three more surgeries made Mann a one-legged shadow of his old self in 1992-93, but he barely missed a game.

"I came back too early after hurting my knee [in 1993] and it ended up costing me," Mann said. "I came back four weeks after having surgery. My wife told me, 'Do not come back. The ship is sinking. Don't jump on.' But how could I not? This guy [Petitbon, then the rookie head coach] doesn't deserve this. Everybody's going down on him. I can't be one of those people. I played on one leg the rest of the season."

Rather than retire at the club's request, Mann asked for his release the following spring. He caught on with San Francisco in September and wound up playing little but earning another Super Bowl ring. As fate would have it, Mann's highlight as a 49er took place at RFK Stadium when he sacked Redskins quarterback Gus Frerotte.

"I remember looking around RFK during my last game as a Redskin," Mann said. "I looked up at all those names around the Hall of Stars and wondered if I would be up there one day. When I came back with the 49ers and got the sack, I looked around again and thought, 'How poetic is this'? We had gone to Deion Sanders' old place in Atlanta and he got booed. The same thing happened to Rickey Jackson in New Orleans and to Gary Plummer in San Diego. When my turn came, I told my teammates, 'They're not going to boo me at RFK.' They said I was crazy. . . . I took a bow after the sack and the fans applauded me. I remember laughing at my teammates on the plane back and saying, 'I told you so.' "

As A Redskin

Position: Defensive end.

Years: 1983-93.

Stats: 82 sacks, 784 tackles.

Greatest season: 14 1/2 sacks and 85 tackles in 1985.

Honors: Pro Bowl, 1987-89, 91.

Today: Sportscaster, WUSA-TV, Washington, D.C.

JOE THEISMANN

Joe Theismann

With one sentence, quarterback Joe Theismann exposed his confidence, ticked off half a team — particularly two quarterbacks — and hatched an image for himself. He swaggered into his first NFL training camp in 1974 confident after a successful three-year stint in the Canadian Football League.

Then he announced, "I'm going to win the starting job."

Never mind that the team already had veterans Sonny Jurgensen and Billy Kilmer. And those two swear what Theismann really said was, "I'm going to put those two old men on the bench."

Thus, a persona was born. After the statement, Jurgensen and Kilmer went from friends to allies, bonding in their dislike of Theismann.

"I know I [upset] them," Theismann said of Jurgensen and Kilmer. "It was just me expressing a belief in my abilities, not a challenge to them like they took it. I regret saying it, but I was just being me. If I was in their shoes, I would have felt the same way and done exactly the same things. [But] to me, if you're not cocky, you can't be the quarterback. If you don't believe you can get the job done, how can others believe in you?"

Receiver Charley Taylor, who liked playing with Theismann, said, "Yeah he was cocky . . . But he needed self-confidence playing behind those two."

Theismann might have annoyed some, but he only wanted to play. He returned punts just to feel as if he was contributing. That season, in an October 20 game against the New York Giants, returner Herb Mul-Key was hurt and backup returner Ken Houston got banged up.

"There was no one else to return punts so I walked up behind coach George [Allen] when he wasn't paying attention and said, 'Kenny's hurt, do you want me to return punts?'" recalled Theismann, who had fielded punts in practice. "George said yes not knowing who it was. I run onto the field and he was like, 'What's he doing out there?' They're yelling at me to get back, but once I stepped foot on the field, I wasn't turning around."

Theismann finished the season with 15 punt returns. Four years later, at age 29, he earned the starting quarterback's job. Four years after that he led the Redskins to a Super Bowl victory. And the team Washington beat in that game was the one that originally drafted Theismann — Miami.

The Dolphins made the Heisman runnerup from Notre Dame a fourth-round pick in 1971, but he didn't want to sit behind Bob Griese and instead signed with Toronto of the CFL. Three years later, Miami traded Theismann's rights to Washington.

Theismann had the longest uninterrupted run as the Redskins' starting quarterback since Hall of Famer Sammy Baugh, who played from 1937-52. Theismann held the job from 1978 to Nov. 18, 1985 when he suffered a career-ending broken right leg versus the Giants.

But he might not have endured if not for a 1981 meeting with then first-year coach Joe Gibbs. After the team started 0-5, Theismann worried about his job status. So he drove to Gibbs' house one night for a chat.

"I felt like he wasn't convinced that I loved football as much as he did," said Theismann, who was only 6-feet and 198 pounds. "I wanted to better understand what he expected of me and to let him know how important football was in my life."

Afterwards, the Redskins played better. They won eight of their next 11 games and over the next three seasons, they finished 39-10 under the athletic Theismann. From 1982-84, there weren't many better quarterbacks. In 1983, he led the Redskins to an NFL-record 541 points. He finished among the top-five rated passers in the NFC for seven straight seasons.

Theismann also rushed for 1,815 yards in his career.

By the time he retired, Theismann had made the complete transformation from a brash kid to a highly-respected teammate.

"Everybody around Joe liked Joe," said center Jeff Bostic. "What I liked is that he exuded confidence. A lot of fans couldn't stand him because of the way he was perceived. [The media] used to say he never saw a microphone he didn't like. But he's one of the most misunderstood people in Redskins' history."

As A Redskin

Position: Quarterback.

Years: 1974-85.

Stats: Redskins career leader in passing yards (25,206), attempts (3,602), completions (2,044). Finished with third-best in Redskins history with 160 touchdowns.

Greatest season: Completed 276 of 459 passes for 3,714 yards and 29 touchdowns in 1983. Also had 97.0 rating, third-best one-season mark in club history.

Honors: Pro Bowl, 1982-83; NFL MVP and Offensive Player-of-the-Year, 1983.

Today: NFL analyst for ESPN; owner, Joe Theismann's Restaurant in Falls Church, Va.

JOE THEISMANN SMILES DESPITE A BROKEN LEG THAT WILL END HIS CAREER.

A Bad Break?

Redskins 23, Giants 21

Pain accompanied his career, inflicting itself at inopportune times. Like in the middle of a game. But it had never stopped quarterback Joe Theismann.

In a way, Theismann liked being injured. Ignore the glamorous looks, prime-time TV appearances and penchant for perfect sound bites. Sure he dashed around town, milking the quarterback's good life. On the field, however, Theismann played tough. And hurt.

In a 1978 Thanksgiving Day game against Dallas, Theismann suffered a deeply bruised chest — an injury as painful as broken ribs — just before halftime. He played the second half.

Three years later, against Dallas, he cracked his right thumb in Joe Gibbs' first game as Washington's coach. Again, Theismann continued to play.

Perhaps nothing topped a December 1982 game versus the New York Giants. In the second quarter, Theismann attempted a quick pass. Linebacker Byron Hunt smashed into him, hitting him underneath the facemask. Because Theismann, who had already thrown three interceptions, didn't wear a mouthpiece despite his single-bar facemask, the blow knocked out two front teeth. He spit out his teeth, called a timeout and huddled with Gibbs.

"I had to convince him I could still talk," Theismann recalled. "It was hard to pronounce things. I had a lisp. He said, 'I'm going to take you out.' I said, 'No, you're not.'

"I had to be careful when I took a deep breath. Anyone with a cavity can appreciate [the pain] when cold air hits it. Here it is late December and I'm trying to suck in hot air."

Gibbs said in the Washington Redskins' Greatest Moments video, "I'm looking at [Joe] and saying, 'Man, if there's a time you take it to the house, it would be right now. Come back and fight another day.'"

But Theismann returned immediately. In the fourth quarter, he threw a key block against cornerback Terry Jackson on a 22-yard Joe Washington touchdown run, which led to a 15-14 victory.

"I saw Joe get stitched up, cut a lip, bust a chin," said tight end Doc Walker. "I always said, 'Wow, what a tough guy.'" To Theismann, that was the ultimate compliment. From 1978, when he became the fulltime starter, to Nov. 18, 1985, Theismann played in every game.

"If someone would ask how I'd like to be remembered, I would hope that my teammates and Redskins fans would say first, 'He's a really tough guy,'" said Theismann, who had his nose broken six times. "And second, 'He did everything he could to help the team win.'"

But 1985 was different.

By then, Theismann had admittedly changed. He was named the NFL's Most Valuable Player in 1983 and afterwards figured he knew it all. When Gibbs would send in a play that called for Theismann to pass outside, the quarterback would sometimes throw over the middle. On plays that called for short passes, Theismann would occasionally throw deep.

It's no wonder 1985 was his worst season. Through 10 games, Theismann was the 13th-rated quarterback — out of 14 — in the NFC thanks to 16 interceptions and last-place marks in passing yards per game (148) and yards per attempt (4.41). He threw five interceptions in a 44-14 season-opening loss at Dallas on his 36th birthday.

At the time, Theismann, who had thrown just eight touchdown passes, refused to believe he had caused his own downfall. But 11 years later, he blamed himself.

"I didn't study as hard, I didn't work as hard," Theismann said. "I was arrogant — people say that I was anyway. I was cocky. I didn't make the commitment to be a football player that I should have. I started to take the game for granted."

But Gibbs had no options. Theismann's backup was 24-year-old Jay Schroeder, who had thrown eight passes in his year-and-a-half as a Redskin and played only two years at UCLA. In Washington, he never took a snap

		1	2	3	4	Total
REDSKINS 23, GIANTS 21						
Giants		7	0	14	0	21
Redskins		7	0	7	9	23

FIRST QUARTER
W — Warren 10 pass from Theismann (Moseley kick), W 7-0
NY — Morris 56 run (Schubert kick), 7-7

THIRD QUARTER
W — Riggins 1 run (Moseley kick), W 14-7
NY — Morris 41 run (Schubert kick), 14-14
NY — Morris 8 run (Schubert kick), NY 21-14

FOURTH QUARTER
W — Moseley 28 FG, NY 21-17
W — Didier 14 pass from Schroeder (kick failed), W 23-21

with the first unit in practice. The former baseball player — he was a catcher in the Toronto organization — wasn't ready to unseat a Pro Bowl passer. Besides, Gibbs had a strong loyalty to his veterans.

The players also stuck by Theismann.

"Joe was playing poorly, but the guy was only two years removed from being the league's MVP," said center Jeff Bostic. "I don't think everyone was locked into saying Jay was ready to take over the reigns."

No change was needed, agreed guard Russ Grimm.

"I'd play with Joe any day," he said. "He's probably one of the greatest competitors I've ever played with. If he missed four passes in a row, it didn't matter. He would complete the fifth one. You talk to people who said they hated him and thought he was cocky, but I loved Joe as a quarterback."

So the 5-5 Redskins stumbled into this 1985 Monday Night game at RFK against New York, winners of four straight and owners of a 7-3 record, including a 17-3 win over Washington in October.

"We're about reaching the end of the road here," Gibbs said before the rematch.

So the fifth-year coach decided tricks were necessary. On its first possession, Washington faced a fourth-and-three after two short Theismann completions. Punter Steve Cox came on, but instead of kicking, he tossed an 11-yard pass to Raphel Cherry for a first down at the New York 46.

After a poorly thrown deep pass to receiver Art Monk, which brought boos from some in the crowd of 53,371, Theismann drove the team downfield. He completed passes to Monk for 11 yards, to receiver Gary Clark for 15 and to tight end Don Warren, in the right flat, for 10 and a touchdown.

New York tied the game two series later when halfback Joe Morris burst through left tackle for a 56-yard touchdown.

Gibbs then resorted to more gimmicks. This time, it was costly. With a first down at the 46, he ordered "50-Gut Throwback." On this play, Riggins takes the hand-off and takes two steps forward, stops, and flips it back to Theismann.

Against the Giants, Theismann took the pitch, looked deep and felt the pocket collapsing. Linebacker Harry Carson and tackle Jim Burt nearly flattened him. Theismann moved to his left. Then linebacker Lawrence Taylor jumped on Theismann from behind. As Theismann fell to his right, Taylor dragged him down and fell on the quarterback's right leg with 14:13 to go in the half.

Snap!

It was gruesome. Theismann's right leg broke between the ankle and the knee. Immediately, Taylor waved to the Redskins' sideline for help.

"I heard a crack," Taylor said after the game. "It went through me. It felt like it happened to me. It made me sick."

Trainer Bubba Tyer and team doctor Charles Jackson raced over from the Washington sideline and knew immediately the leg was broken. It was an easy diagnosis as the tibia had torn the skin. When Tyer saw Theismann's blood-soaked sock, he knew it was a compound fracture.

Ironically, Theismann wasn't in hysterics.

"The worse the injury is, the calmer the players are," Tyer said. "Their bodies go into shock."

They placed Theismann's leg in a splint, put him on a stretcher and wheeled him off the field. First, though, Theismann asked Tyer for a favor.

"Get to a phone, call my mother and tell her I'm OK," Theismann told him.

Players huddled around Theismann and offered their good wishes. Cornerback Darrell Green came over and held his hand for a spell as did Theismann's card-playing partner and good friend, guard Mark May.

Bostic remembered seeing Giants vomiting on the field.

Then, as Theismann was leaving, he yelled to Carson.

"Harry, I understand you're thinking about retiring," Theismann remembered saying. "He said, 'Yes I am.' I said, 'Well don't you go retiring because I'm coming back.'"

But Carson provided the zinger: "That may be the case, pal. But it ain't going to be tonight."

Finally, Theismann turned to Schroeder and implored him to get the job done. Then it was over. The crowd erupted in an ovation for Theismann, who was joined in the tunnel by actress girlfriend Cathy Lee Crosby.

An ambulance took Theismann to Arlington Hospital, where he wouldn't let them operate until the game ended. A black-and-white TV, using a hanger to provide better reception, was set up outside the window of the preparatory room. Theismann cheered from his bed.

What he, and the nation, saw was a calm Schroeder — who said he only gets nervous when his wife is having a baby — taking over. The transition happened on his second play – before Theismann had reached the end of the tunnel. Schroeder whipped a 44-yard pass to Monk at the New York 13.

"When that ball took off, everybody on the sidelines jumped," Gibbs said. "Everybody said, 'Hey, we may take a run at this.'"

May said, "After that pass, the torch was passed."

Two runs moved the ball nine yards, but on third-and-one, Riggins fumbled and Taylor recovered.

Washington didn't score again and the half ended with the teams tied at 7. But Schroeder had eased the fears of his teammates.

"I had never been more uncertain what one of my teammates might do," Bostic said. "But after Jay threw a couple balls, it didn't take you long to realize this guy [could play]."

At halftime, Gibbs asked Schroeder if he wanted him to scale back the offense. Schroeder, saying it was easier for one player to change than an entire offense, answered no.

Schroeder was ready. And it didn't take him long to break the tie. Cox executed an onside kick to start the second half and recovered the ball himself as the Giants had turned to race back. Schroeder quickly hit Monk (who would finish with seven catches for 130 yards) for 50 yards to the Giants' 4-yard line. Three plays later Riggins scored from the 1.

Morris tied the score on the ensuing series with a 41-yard run. Riggins fumbled again, but the defense stopped New York on a fourth-and-one at the Redskins' 24. However, fullback George Rogers fumbled the ball back to the Giants on his own 23. Morris made it 21-14 with an 8-yard touchdown run.

Mark Moseley's 28-yard field goal, capping a 65-yard drive, cut the deficit to four with 11:25 left. The drive featured second-year running back Keith Griffin, who entered in place of the fumbling Riggins and Rogers. Griffin's fumbling problems had nearly cost him a roster spot, but he provided a spark against the Giants with 15 carries for 44 yards and three receptions for 27 more.

Following the field goal, Gibbs felt lucky again as he ordered yet another onside kick. Once more the gamble worked as Greg Williams pounced on the loose ball at the New York 46.

Five plays later, Schroeder fired a pass that cornerback Elvis Patterson tipped into the hands of tight end Clint Didier for a 14-yard score. But Moseley's missed extra point attempt left the score 23-21 with 8:21 remaining.

The Redskins' defense took it from there as New York struggled to mount an attack after Didier's touchdown. The Giants couldn't even cross the 50.

"We were Buster Douglas that day," said linebacker Monte Coleman. "And we just beat Mike Tyson."

Thanks to Schroeder. He had done the job, completing 13-of-20 passes for 221 yards against the NFC's top-ranked defense.

"I just knew it was going to happen sometime," Schroeder said, "whether it was this year, next year or the year after."

He became an instant celebrity. The following morning, Schroeder spent the day recounting his story. In between the interviews, which started at 7 a.m. on a local radio show, he sped home for his son's first birthday.

Schroeder would finish the season with 1,458 passing yards, five touchdowns and five interceptions. The Redskins, with a 5-1 record under Schroeder, wound up 10-6 and missed the playoffs because of tiebreakers.

Meanwhile, Theismann's injury was replayed countless times. He watched the play a few days later. Once. Teammates viewed it as many times as they could stand.

"I couldn't wait to get home to see it on TV," said defensive end Charles Mann. "My wife [Tyreena] was like, 'No, how can we?' But we both sat there and watched it. She watched it once. I watched it five or six times. I'm not grossed out by things."

Just four days after the injury, Theismann publicly vowed to return. When Gibbs asked Theismann to retire in January, the quarterback declined. So for half a year, he rehabilitated the leg, but made little progress. Finally, in July, Theismann drove to Jack Kent Cooke's farm in Middleburg, Va., where the Redskins' owner asked him to retire or be waived. Theismann didn't want to quit, so he was waived.

"That night I cried," he said.

In November, nearly a year after the injury, Theismann retired.

Perhaps a change at quarterback was needed. But few were happy to see Theismann leave.

"To me, he was my only quarterback," Coleman said.

Theismann wasn't ready to relinquish his job and for three years he suffered withdrawal pains from football. After his injury, he realized how important the sport was to him. But don't think his last moment on the field was an unhappy one. The ovation Theismann received as he left on the stretcher still rings in his ears.

"I do a lot of motivational speaking and the one thing I recognize in my speeches is the appreciation that I have for the people at RFK that night," Theismann said. "They weren't applauding anything I did on the football field. They were thanking a man, a man who thought he didn't need anybody. That ovation changed my life. RFK was more than a place to pursue my work, RFK was a place of salvation for me."

Jay Schroeder doesn't waste time showing his teammates he belongs.

ART MONK

Art Monk

When Art Monk left the Redskins in the spring of 1994, he was the leading receiver in NFL history with 888 catches. He had helped lead Washington to three Super Bowl titles and eight playoff berths in his 14 seasons. Not bad production for a man who said, "I couldn't catch the ball to save my life when I got to Syracuse."

But those who knew the quiet Monk don't mention the gorgeous catches he made or the crunching blocks he threw when they're asked to explain his greatness. They talk about his approach to the game.

"Art's still the greatest as far as I'm concerned," said center Raleigh McKenzie, a teammate for nine seasons. "He treated football as his love and livelihood. He didn't slack off in anything he did: running, lifting, studying. If you had a monitor on Art 365 days a year, you'd say, 'That's a true football player and a true man.' "

Added defensive end Charles Mann, a teammate for 11 years, "Art was always in the best shape; not the most muscular or the strongest, just the best shape. You would hardly ever see Art sweat. Art's a self-motivator."

That wasn't always true. Monk had been a fine athlete at Syracuse — where he started out as a halfback — but he honed those skills through hard work once he reached the NFL.

"[Veteran Redskins halfback] Terry Metcalf lived across the street from me during my second season and all we did from the time we got up until we went to sleep was train and compete," Monk said. "It would be 9 a.m. in February and Terry would be dragging me out for a bike ride. That's what really got my workout discipline started."

That regimen didn't slack off when Monk found himself out of the NFL in 1996, having not been re-signed by a third team in two years. Although he was 38 and coming off a broken arm he suffered after being picked up by Philadelphia in November 1995, Monk was still hoping to play a 17th season in 1996. Monk didn't just want the 60 catches he needed to reach 1,000. He has a fearsome desire to compete.

"The younger guys [Gary Clark and Ricky Sanders] would get us down the field, but whenever we needed a clutch play, we looked to Art," said Mark Rypien, the quarterback during Monk's final five Redskins seasons. "No. 81 was going to get the ball. He was the go-to guy."

That was true from the April day in 1980 when Washington made Monk its first No. 1 pick in 12 years. Although he didn't become a starter until midseason, Monk still led the team with a Redskins rookie record 58 catches. His 894 yards the following season were the most by a Washington receiver in 14 years. The players' strike and injuries curtailed his 1982 and 1983 seasons, but Monk rebounded dramatically in 1984, setting a then-NFL season record with 106 catches.

Monk was five catches behind Charley Hennigan's record going into the season finale against St. Louis. Washington needed to win to capture the NFC East title. Late in the game with the record in hand but the Redskins trailing, 27-26, Monk made his biggest play, grabbing Joe Theismann's third-and-19 pass right at the down marker. It was Monk's 11th catch of the day. Moments later, Mark Moseley kicked the game-winning, division-clinching 37-yard field goal.

"A lot of guys have it backwards," Monk explained. "They want to do well and hope their team does well. I believed that if the team played well, the individual things would take care of themselves."

Clark, who made the tough catches over the middle, and deep threat Sanders each made well over 600 career catches but still fell far short of Monk. He was the master of the down-and-out pattern. Opposing cornerbacks knew what was coming, but they couldn't stop it.

"Art had a flair for consistency," Theismann said. "I've never known a greater football player."

Monk followed his record-setting 1984 season by averaging 77 catches over his next six full years (another strike and injuries limited him in 1987). So he entered 1992 just 18 catches shy of Steve Largent's all-time NFL record. Monk broke it in a Monday night blowout of Denver on one of his typical 10-yard down-and-outs before being hoisted on his teammates' shoulders as the RFK Stadium crowd saluted him wildly.

"It was real heartwarming to play your games at RFK," said Monk, arguably the most popular Redskin ever. "I was really hoping I would break the record at home. I couldn't have asked for a better feeling."

The feeling was mutual.

"Art could be mayor of D.C. without anyone knowing anything about his political persuasion," said tight end Terry Orr. "I played with Art and I trained with him in the offseason, but even I have his autograph."

MONTE COLEMAN

Monte Coleman

Monte Coleman wasn't destined for a record-setting Redskins career.

The son of a teacher and a railroad worker from Pine Bluff, Ark., Coleman walked on at Central Arkansas as a receiver in 1975 having played just one high school varsity game. Put at cornerback for a junior varsity college game, Coleman picked off three passes, one for a touchdown, and a defensive career was born. He played safety on the NAIA champions as a sophomore. But the skinny Coleman was still there for Washington, 11 rounds and 289 picks into the 1979 draft.

"I wasn't intimidated and I wasn't worried about making the team," said Coleman, who had a wife and son and whose signing bonus was just $7,000. "I told myself I was going to play as hard as I could and study as much as I could and let the chips fall where they may. I still remember when they came to get my roommate, Tony Hall, to tell him he had been cut. My locker was next to Olky's [rookie free agent linebacker Neal Olkewicz, who would play 11 seasons]. Every day there would be another empty locker in the room and we would wonder who would be next."

Countless faces filled the nearby lockers over the years, but Coleman remained to play under coaches Jack Pardee, Joe Gibbs, Richie Petitbon and Norv Turner. He started alongside players ranging from Coy Bacon, who was born in 1943, to Tom Carter, who was born in 1972.

"Monte had no idea what was going on as far as sophisticated football when we drafted him, but he could do something no one else could do – he could cover backs out of the backfield man-to-man," Petitbon said. "He developed into the best nickel linebacker they ever made."

Coleman played so long, he took part in half of the club's 32 training camps in Carlisle, Pa. Only Hall of Fame quarterback Sammy Baugh lasted as many seasons as Coleman's 16. Although he averaged fewer than four starts during those 16 years, Coleman played in a record 216 games for the Redskins.

"My career kind of typifies that era from 1982-92 when the Redskins were so great," Coleman said. "I was an 11th-round draft choice who wasn't supposed to make it, let alone play 16 years. We weren't supposed to win three Super Bowls and make the playoffs eight times. But we had guys who worked hard and knew what it took."

That was Coleman. He was blessed with speed and size, but few players worked as hard at staying in shape, especially after a series of injuries kept him out of 22 games in his first eight years. During Coleman's final season, 1994, his 37-year-old body was as chiseled as 29-year-old Pro Bowl linebacker Ken Harvey's. No wonder his teammates called Coleman "Superman."

Only linemen Dexter Manley, Charles Mann and Dave Butz had more sacks for the Redskins than Coleman's 56 1/2 and only cornerback Darrell Green returned more interceptions for touchdowns than Coleman's three.

"If it was an easy play, Monte wasn't going to make it," Mann said, "but if he had to crawl on the ground and reach up to grab the ball out of the quarterback's hand or one-hand an interception that was just about to hit the ground, Monte would do that."

Many players with that kind of ability would have groused about not starting, but Coleman knew his limited role caused his body less wear and tear and extended his career. He thrived as the third-down linebacker, excelling both in pass rush and pass coverage.

"I loved Monte," said Larry Pecatiello, Coleman's position coach for 13 years. "He was the consummate team player. Monte was good enough to start on most teams, but he took a lot of pride in his role."

Besides, complaining wasn't the beloved Coleman's style.

"Monte's always upbeat," linebacker Kurt Gouveia said during Coleman's final season. "When you're down, he'll pick you up. If you need someone to hang onto, Monte will be there for you."

Coleman's dedication was on display on Dec. 19, 1993, in a meaningless game against Atlanta. Starting for just the fifth time in the 1990s, Coleman returned a fumble for a touchdown, picked off a pass, made two sacks and forced a fumble to lead Washington to a rare victory.

"The highest compliment you can give a player was to call him a pro," said Mike Haluchak, Coleman's last position coach. "Monte was a pro."

And a Redskin.

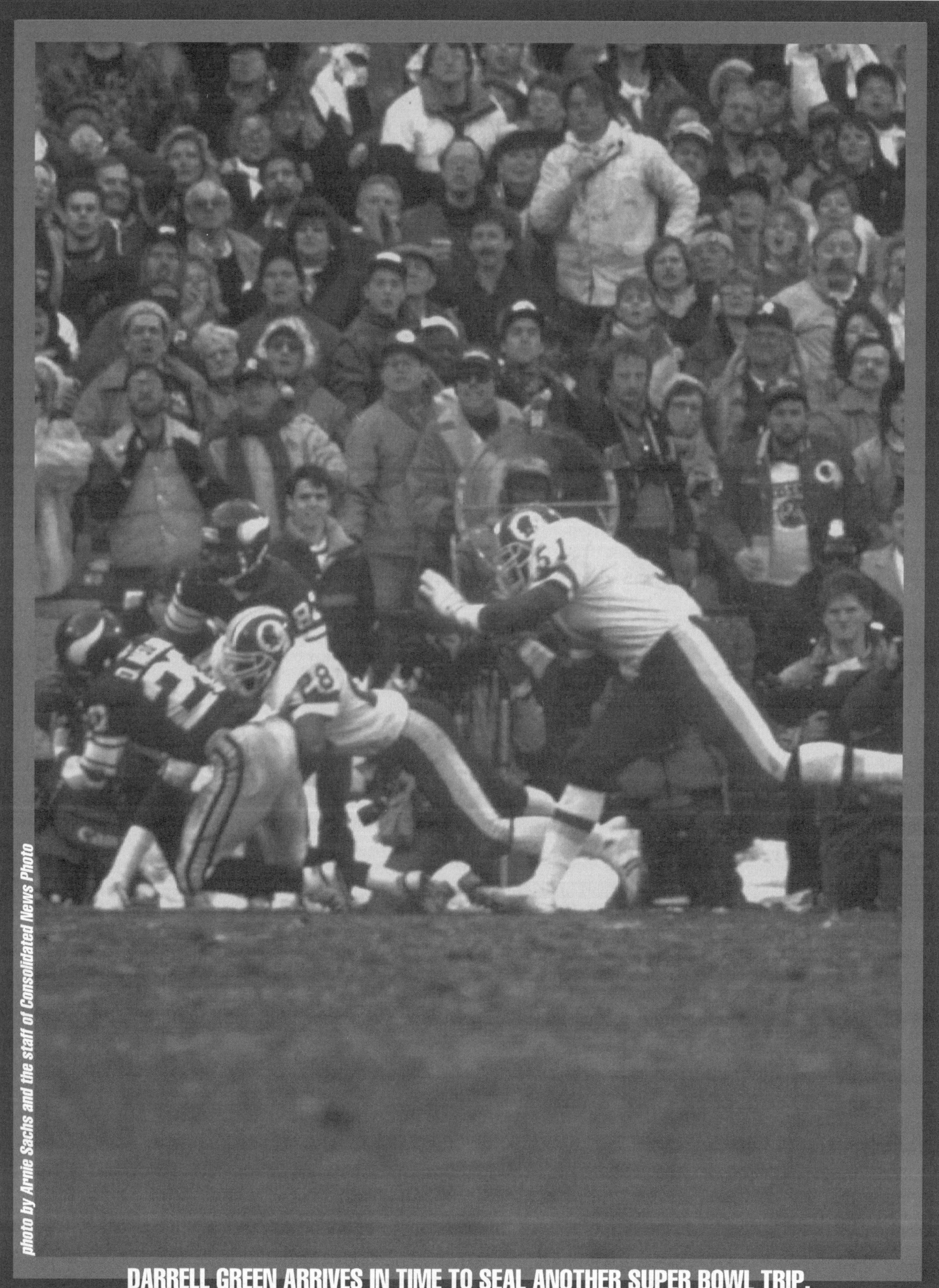

DARRELL GREEN ARRIVES IN TIME TO SEAL ANOTHER SUPER BOWL TRIP.

Super Close

Redskins 17, Vikings 10

It was the strangest of seasons, 1987.

As in 1982, a players' strike disrupted the season. But unlike the debacle which canceled seven of the 16 games five years before, this time, the owners were prepared. They quickly formed replacement teams and had them in action after canceling just one week of games.

It would have been a strange year in Washington even without the strike. Offensive line mainstays Russ Grimm and Mark May got hurt. So did star receiver Art Monk, who cost the Redskins a game by dropping a sure touchdown pass. Linebacker Monte Coleman, a backup for the previous five seasons and the next seven, *started* in 1987.

Coach Joe Gibbs wavered between quarterbacks Jay Schroeder and Doug Williams all year. Cornerback Barry Wilburn came out of nowhere to lead the NFL in interceptions. Washington lost to lowly Atlanta but beat nemesis Dallas twice for just the second time in club history.

"It was an ugly year," Monk said. "It's hard to explain."

The crazy season started in Philadelphia. Schroeder, Grimm, kicker Jess Atkinson and running back George Rogers all got hurt, but Williams — who hadn't thrown a pass the year before — came off the bench to lead a 34-24 victory with 272 yards and two touchdowns.

The roller coaster ride began the following week in Atlanta, where the Falcons, coming off a 48-10 embarrassment to Tampa Bay, won a seesaw struggle 21-20 helped by Bostic's snapping the ball over holder Eric Yarber's head on an extra point attempt by new kicker Ali Haji-Sheikh.

Then came the strike. General manager Bobby Beathard and his assistant, Charley Casserly, needed just 10 days to put together a decent replacement team. Better than decent. Much better.

"Anytime there was upheaval in the league, the strikes, the USFL, to me that was the time of greatest opportunity," said Gibbs, whose team had won the Super Bowl during the strike-shortened 1982 season and which had received a talent transfusion in 1986 with the addition of receivers Gary Clark and Ricky Sanders and running back Kelvin Bryant from the USFL. "Chances are, with all of that going on a lot of people don't handle that very well. If you can handle it better than anybody else, you've got a better chance to accomplish what you want."

Unlike many teams which split over labor issues, Washington's regulars all went out on strike. That togetherness could be dangerous - defensive tackle Darryl Grant smashed a window in the bus carrying the replacement players - but it paid off during and after the strike.

The new Redskins first faced a St. Louis team with more than 10 regular players. Led by three touchdown passes from Ed Rubbert to Anthony Allen (who joined cornerback Dennis Woodberry in remaining Redskins after the strike), Washington won 28-21 at RFK.

The replacements then did something the regulars couldn't do in three tries in 1986, beat the New York Giants, although not the real ones.

That 38-12 triumph sent Washington to Dallas. It was Monday, Oct. 19, 1987 — the day of the worst stock market slide in 58 years — and the Cowboys, with such stars as Tony Dorsett, Randy White and Danny White in the lineup, were in for just as rude an awakening.

REDSKINS 17, VIKINGS 10					
	1	2	3	4	Total
Vikings	0	7	0	3	10
Redskins	7	0	3	7	17

FIRST QUARTER
W - Bryant 43 pass from Williams (Haji-Sheikh kick), W 7-0
SECOND QUARTER
M - Lewis 23 pass from Wilson (C. Nelson kick), 7-7
THIRD QUARTER
W - Haji-Sheikh 28 FG, W 10-7
FOURTH QUARTER
M - C. Nelson 18 FG, 10-10
W - Clark 7 pass from Williams (Haji-Sheikh kick), W 17-10

"A lot of people make a lot out of that game, but I think that it was a disadvantage to have your veterans in there because they weren't going to accept those strike guys," Gibbs said. "Our deal was much better. They were all strike players. They loved each other."

Many of the Redskins players gathered at ex-teammate Doc Walker's restaurant to watch the game. They were as incredulous as anyone when their replacements, led by backup quarterback Tony Robinson, H-back Craig McEwen and running back Lionel Vital, stunned the Cowboys, 13-7.

"I appreciated the fact that they won for us, but the fact that they were in there taking our place wasn't right," Monk said.

"We can't argue that Bobby Beathard, Charley Casserly and coach Gibbs had an eye for talent," Coleman said, still referring to the replacements as "scabs" almost a decade later.

Maybe returning with an NFC-leading 5-1 record assuaged some of the regulars' anger. Whatever the case, Schroeder's sprained left shoulder had healed and he started against the New York Jets. But veteran defensive tackle Dave Butz provided the inspiration. He crawled out of a hospital bed minus 24 pounds courtesy of an intestinal virus – to record the clutch fourth-quarter sack and set up Haji-Sheikh's 28-yard field goal which pulled out a 17-16 victory.

Washington then thumped Buffalo, and after losing to Philadelphia on Randall Cunningham's last-minute bomb to Greg Garrity, edged Detroit as Green intercepted three passes and Williams relieved Schroeder again. Next came Monk's rare end-zone gaffe which cost the Redskins a victory over the Los Angeles Rams.

Washington was 8-3 heading into a Thanksgiving weekend showdown with New York. The Giants were just 3-7, but they led 16-0 at halftime in front of a stunned RFK crowd.

"We were in deep, deep trouble," Gibbs said.

Schroeder, back at quarterback for the third time in the wake of Williams' sprained back, led the comeback with the seventh 300-yard day of his two-year career. Schroeder's third touchdown pass in 12 minutes, a 28-yarder to Sanders with 4:56 left, gave Washington a 23-19 lead, but victory wasn't assured until the defense stopped halfback Tony Galbreath at the 2 as time ran out.

The following week's 34-17 rout of the Cardinals clinched the NFC East title. The Redskins then held on to beat Dallas and failed to hold off a rally by host Miami. In the season finale at Minnesota, with the offense scoreless at halftime of a 7-7 game, Gibbs yanked Schroeder for Williams. The Vikings led 24-14 before the Redskins roared back, winning 27-24 on Haji-Sheikh's 26-yard field goal in overtime.

For the second straight year, the Redskins ventured to Chicago for a playoff game and for the second straight year, they won. Despite frigid conditions — "That was the coldest I've ever been. The Vaseline froze to my body," said defensive end Charles Mann — and a 14-0 deficit, Washington overcame the odds and the powerful Bears.

Green, who returned a punt 52 yards for the winning touchdown despite tearing rib cartilage while hurdling a Bear, was the hero of the 21-17 victory.

"It was just instinctive," Green said. "That was all I could do."

Green would be proven wrong in the following week's NFC Championship Game against Minnesota.

"The thing we had going for us was a psychological edge," Mann said. "We had never lost to Minnesota [in four games under Gibbs]."

But the Vikings were on fire.

"No one gave us a chance the way they had demolished New Orleans and San Francisco," McKenzie remembered. "But our defense shocked them and kept them in the fold. And we did what a lot of teams couldn't do against them: we ran the football."

And not with leading rusher Rogers or the elusive Bryant carrying it. Rookie Timmy Smith was the main man, gaining 72 yards - just four less than the entire Minnesota team - on only 13 carries.

But the Redskins still scored just once in the first half as Bryant beat linebacker Jesse Solomon for a 42-yard touchdown catch. On the opening drive, Haji-Sheikh missed field goal tries from 38 and 47 yards. Clark dropped a ball in the end zone, prompting Minnesota's game-tying touchdown drive which ended when Leo Lewis beat Wilburn and grabbed a 23-yard pass from Wade Wilson. Williams — who didn't leave the game despite bruising his right shoulder — overthrew Clark on another sure Washington score.

"I didn't get discouraged if the offense wasn't scoring," said Redskins linebacker Mel Kaufman. "We just had to do our job, stop the other team from scoring and keep giving the offense opportunities."

Kaufman did that with an interception off a deflection by Butz which set up Haji-Sheikh's go-ahead 28-yard field goal in the third quarter.

Defensive coordinator Richie Petitbon seemingly threw the entire playbook at the Vikings, who had scored 80 points against the Saints and 49ers. Petitbon used fronts of three, four and five men and even put backup linebacker Ravin Caldwell inside of the ends.

"They were moving people around and we had some confusions with our blocking patterns," said Minnesota coach Jerry Burns, whose line allowed six sacks before halftime.

"The best way to play pass defense is to have the quarterback on his can," Petitbon said with typical bluntness. "Our defense is a little better than average, [but] the guys play hard and we probably get the most out of what we have."

They had to on this day because Williams (9-for-26, 119 yards) was badly off-target.

After two big plays by receiver Anthony Carter put the Vikings in Washington territory, middle linebacker Neal Olkewicz became the first game-saver. Olkewicz dove across the pile on third-and-goal to thwart halfback D.J. Dozier inches short of the end zone with less than 11 minutes left.

"When you go for a play like that, you can't stop in the middle and I think D.J. did," Wilson said.

Burns declined to take another shot at the touchdown, and Chuck Nelson kicked the game-tying 18-yard field goal. But Clark beat Reggie Rutland for 43 yards to set up

his own 7-yard touchdown catch on a broken pattern which Williams smartly read the same way. Washington led 17-10 with 5:15 to go.

Wilson responded by hitting 5-of-6 passes, the last one of which put the Vikings on the Washington 6 with 1:05 left.

"The whole way downfield, we were like, 'C'mon guys, c'mon defense, you're better than that,' " Monk said of the sideline mood.

"There was a lot of talk in the huddle," Mann said. "Not confusion, but a lot of people saying what we needed to do. Everybody was making adjustments mentally and expressing them verbally so we were all on the same page."

Wilson threw an incompletion on second down and Mann pressured him into a hurried throw on the next play. It was fourth-and-the-season with 56 seconds remaining. Gibbs knelt in prayer.

Minnesota called 83-Option-Smoke. Carter was supposed to clear the left side for a pass to halfback Darrin Nelson, but he didn't run his pattern deep enough so even though Nelson had faked Coleman out, Green – who almost didn't play before finally squaring his conscience with a pain-killing pre-game shot to his ribs – was in position.

"They tried to reverse the thinking, saying, 'I know he's going to think it's coming to Anthony Carter, but we're going to clear that side out,' " Green recalled. "The problem is: how much can you clear out on the 6-yard line? The play developed slowly. I let Anthony go to the back of the end zone. I went full speed ahead."

Just as Nelson touched the ball at the goal line, Green arrived.

"I had my hands on it," Nelson said. "Anytime you have your hands on the ball, you ought to catch it."

But he didn't and the Redskins went wild with joy.

"I looked like I was a hero; everybody thought I knocked it out, but Nelson wouldn't have caught the ball anyway," Green said.

The Redskins had reached their third Super Bowl in six years, but Green wasn't going to have to be heroic again. Smith's record 204 yards on 22 carries, Sanders' nine catches for 193 yards and Williams' 340 yards and four touchdown passes which keyed a record 35-point second quarter were plenty. Washington crushed Denver 42-10.

DOUG WILLIAMS

Doug Williams

If football players are stars, then Doug Williams was a meteorite. The quarterback only played in 22 games over four seasons in Washington, but one quarter made his stay worthwhile.

Williams gained his 15 minutes of fame when it mattered — before a worldwide audience. Down 10-0, Williams led five straight touchdown drives, including four scoring passes, for a 35-10 second-quarter lead over the Denver Broncos en route to a 42-10 victory in Super Bowl XXII. Williams was named the Most Valuable Player after setting Super Bowl records for most passing yards (340), passing yards in a quarter (228), touchdown passes (4) and longest completion (80). Not bad for a quarterback who began the season as a backup, started only two regular season games and was just two years away from retirement.

"They say everybody is famous for 15 minutes," Williams said. "I guess I had mine. For that quarter, we executed better than anybody in the history of football."

Williams was equally influential off the field. The Super Bowl is a media circus where more than 2,000 reporters often ask the same questions. However, one stuck out.

"How long have you been a black quarterback," Williams was asked by a tongue-tied reporter.

Williams was good humored enough to say all of his life. But the question cut deep. The race card was about to be played in public. A first-round selection in 1978 by the Tampa Bay Buccaneers, Williams received sacks of hate mail — including a rotten watermelon after a loss — from people wanting him to die simply for being black. No matter how many games he won — and Tampa Bay's only playoff appearances were in 1979 and 1981-82 with Williams starting — it was never enough to win over Bucs fans before he jumped to the USFL in 1983.

Now Williams would become the first black quarterback to start in the Super Bowl, and he knew everyone was watching.

"Yes, black America was watching me," he said. "I knew that, but I was not going to my room at night thinking about what people were asking me. I was thinking about how to beat the Broncos."

In the second quarter alone, Williams completed 9-of-11 passes for 228 yards with touchdown passes of 88, 27, 50 and 8 yards. He finished the game 18-of-29 for 340 yards. After hyperextending his left knee late in the first quarter, Williams refused to leave for more than a play.

"Everyone had confidence in Doug," said offensive linemen Raleigh McKenzie. "You knew he had been through it all. There were people fussing, and he handled it well."

Williams played 11 games in 1988, but he was already fading from the spotlight. An appendicitis attack forced him to miss four games in 1989 and begin the transition to Mark Rypien, who would become the starter.

"My stay in Washington was too short," Williams said. "When I think about my football career, I spent five useless years in Tampa. I wish I could have spent the whole time in Washington."

Said center Jeff Bostic: "Doug probably had one of the purest passing arms I ever saw. When he got to us, his body was beat up."

Added tight end Terry Orr: "He threw the best pass I've ever seen. No one threw an easier pass to catch."

Williams' stay in Washington was short but sweet, and with an impact on football that extended beyond RFK. Williams doesn't know whether his career will have a long-lasting effect on opportunities for black quarterbacks, but he knows everyone now pays attention to the subject.

"I never really sat down and thought about what I did for black America," he said. "I didn't see the Joe Louis-Max Schmeling fight. I didn't see Jackie Robinson steal home so I can't picture what I've done.

"What did I change? Nothing. If there were 10 or 12 black quarterbacks in the NFL, some black backups and third-teamers, then I'd think I changed something. The NFL would still rather draft a [white] guy from Slippery Rock than give a black quarterback a chance. Maybe I'll feel I've made a difference when [a former black head coach such as] Art Shell wins the Super Bowl."

As A Redskin

Position: Quarterback.

Years: 1986-89.

Stats: Completed 345 of 617 passes for 4,350 yards and 27 touchdowns.

Greatest season: Completed 213 of 380 passes for 2,609 yards and 15 touchdowns in 1988.

Honors: Most Valuable Player, Super Bowl XXII.

Today: Jacksonville Jaguars scout.

DARRELL GREEN

Darrell Green

From out of nowhere the rookie darted, chasing down a legend and creating his own. Darrell Green, in his first NFL game, caught Dallas running back Tony Dorsett from behind. A nationwide audience, watching this Monday Night game Sept. 5, 1983 at RFK Stadium, gasped. The speedy Dorsett had busted off a 77-yard run and raced toward the end zone. Until Green appeared.

"I was on the ground and all of a sudden this missile goes by me," said Washington linebacker Mel Kaufman. "I said, 'What was that?' "

Sometimes Green wishes it hadn't happened. He had fallen into a speed trap.

"When I came into the league, I had two chips on my shoulder," Green said. " 'He's too little and he's fast.' I wanted to be recognized as a covering cornerback. The first thing I did was run down Tony Dorsett. That was the wrong thing to do and it extended that thinking of, 'Boy, he can run.'

"It took me years to overcome that. Fortunately, I not only overcame that one-dimensional thinking, but I also maintained the speed. In the beginning, it was tough and I fought against that. I didn't want to be known as just a fast guy."

But when you run the 40-yard dash in 4.2 seconds — and win the NFL's Fastest Man Competition three times — that's what happens. However, speed alone doesn't make someone the top cornerback in the league, which Green was during his prime. The Redskins matched him against the other team's top receiver, and never worried about the 5-foot-8, 184-pound Green.

He was a first-round pick out of Division II Texas A&I, but the coaches didn't hesitate to start him as a rookie when Jeris White held out and later quit.

"I would like to have worked [Green] in slower," recalled defensive coordinator Richie Petitbon. "But it became evident early on that this is a kid who didn't need to get his feet wet. He had a tremendous belief in himself and went strictly on physical ability. As he picked up techniques, he got better and better. He was as fast as anyone I ever coached.

"Darrell probably had as much to do with the success of the Redskins in the '80s and '90s as anybody. He could take the best receiver out of the game with no help and enabled us to do more blitzing than normal. He's one of the best cover guys I've ever seen."

Green said his first season could be broken in half. The first eight games tested his psyche as teams picked on him. But in the second half, Green said he played at an all-Pro level.

And the reason Green succeeded, despite a rocky start, is what sets him apart — his ability to forget.

"That's just from being a little bitty kid all my life," Green said. "Every battle I was in, I was outmatched in size. You learn to find resolve. I don't worry that he beat me. I'm still thinking about what I have in mind. And I have in mind to beat him. The other thing is, you're a professional and you're paid to do a job. You've got four quarters to do it. There's not enough time to freak out."

Green is a fixture in the community thanks in part to the Darrell Green Youth Life Foundation as well as his personality. He's also a rarity because few cornerbacks last as long as Green.

As for on-field highlights, Green has had so many, it's difficult to single them out. Some are worth remembering like the 72-yard interception return for a touchdown in the playoffs as a rookie against the Rams; the three interceptions against Detroit in 1987; the interception returns for scores against Detroit in the 1991 NFC Championship and versus Buffalo in the Super Bowl two weeks later. Another interception return — his franchise-record fourth — beat the Lions in overtime in 1995.

There was also the 52-yard punt return that helped beat Chicago in the 1987 playoffs. Green tore rib cartilage on the play.

"It felt like someone was putting a match on my ribs," Green said. "You talk about hurting."

But he played the following week and defended the last-second pass to Minnesota's Darrin Nelson in the NFC Championship Game.

Four years later the entire season was a highlight.

"In 1991, they couldn't even complete a ball on me in practice," Green said. "There were a few years where, in my mind, no one could beat me."

But even if they did, the chase wasn't over. That's what Dorsett — and the nation — learned long ago.

RICKY ERVINS AND THE HOGS SHOW ATLANTA WHO OWNS THE DAY.

The Seat Cushion Game

Redskins 24, Falcons 7

The 1991 season didn't start off with great omens for the Redskins.

Mark Rypien, facing a challenge from Stan Humphries for the starting quarterback job he had owned for two years, held out for the first 10 days of training camp. Then, tight end Don Warren, a blocking machine, broke his ankle and was lost until midseason. To top it off, the Redskins went 1-3 in preseason.

That all had Joe Gibbs fretting more than usual, but even the worrywart coach couldn't deny that he had a talented, veteran team.

"That was the most tight-knit team I ever had and the easiest to coach," Gibbs said.

Art Monk, Gary Clark and Ricky Sanders were the NFL's top trio of receivers. Running back Earnest Byner had averaged more than 1,000 yards the past three seasons. Original Hogs Joe Jacoby, Russ Grimm and Jeff Bostic had been complemented by Jim Lachey and Mark Schlereth. Kicker Chip Lohmiller was among the league's best.

End Charles Mann, linebacker Wilber Marshall and cornerback Darrell Green led a defense which the year before had been Washington's stingiest since 1982. Safety Todd Bowles and middle linebacker Greg Manusky had departed as Plan B free agents but had been replaced by Danny Copeland and Matt Millen, who arrived via the same route.

"I played golf with Ricky Sanders and [defensive backs coach] Emmitt Thomas before the season started and Emmitt said, 'We're going to win the Super Bowl if we don't screw it up,' " said tight end Terry Orr.

The Redskins, who had been to the Super Bowl three times from 1982-87, had won just one playoff game since. But they had trailed host San Francisco by just a touchdown in the fourth quarter the previous January before losing 26-13. That defeat seemed to galvanize Washington's veterans for one last collective title push in 1991.

"It was almost like everybody took a blood oath before the season that we weren't going to leave a fellow player behind," Mann said.

Said Rypien, "We probably weren't the most talented team. What we had was a lot of guys who played hard and had a tremendous amount of knowledge about the game. A lot of the guys [nine] had played 10-12 years. They knew how to win. We could get the gameplan on Wednesday and spit it out almost perfectly on Sunday."

That perfection began on Labor Day weekend. Detroit's all-Pro halfback Barry Sanders was injured, but Washington showed no sympathy, registering its 15th straight victory over the visiting Lions by a resounding 45-0.

The Redskins received a similar break the next week at Dallas when Cowboys halfback Emmitt Smith, who had scampered 75 yards through Washington's befuddled defense for a touchdown and had caught a scoring pass to make it 21-10, left the game with severe dehydration. Lohmiller's 52-yard field goal just before halftime pulled the Redskins within 21-20.

Lohmiller, who would hit four kicks from 45 yards or beyond, wasn't the only special teams star. Halfback Brian Mitchell's 3-yard run on a fourth-and-one fake punt midway through the fourth quarter set up fullback Gerald Riggs' touchdown dive which put Washington

	1	2	3	4	Total
REDSKINS 24, FALCONS 7					
Falcons	0	7	0	0	7
Redskins	0	14	3	7	24

SECOND QUARTER
W - Ervins 17 run (Lohmiller kick), W 7-0
W - Riggs 2 run (Lohmiller kick), W 14-0
A - T. Johnson 1 run (N. Johnson kick), W 14-7

THIRD QUARTER
W   Lohmiller 24 FG, W 17-7

FOURTH QUARTER
W - Riggs 1 run (Lohmiller kick), W 24-7

ahead to stay in the huge 33-31 triumph.

The home rout, road squeaker pattern followed the next six weeks against Phoenix and Cincinnati, Philadelphia and Chicago [late interceptions broke the game open], Cleveland and the New York Giants. By midseason, Washington was a perfect 8-0, prompting safety Brad Edwards to say, "It was a season where everything went right for us. There was just a magic brewing."

The magic struck again in Week 9 at RFK as kicker Ian Howfield of 7-1 Houston hooked his 34-yard game-winning field goal try with 1:41 to go. Lohmiller's 41-yarder 4:01 into overtime pulled out the victory for the Redskins, who destroyed Atlanta and Pittsburgh the next two weeks behind nine touchdown passes by the red-hot Rypien.

At 11-0, there was talk about surpassing Miami's 14-0 season of 1972 by going 16-0. Dallas dashed those dreams, jumping to a 21-7 lead and holding on to win 24-21 at RFK. Washington rebounded the next week against the Los Angeles Rams before rallying to prevail at Phoenix and crushing the Giants at home. Gibbs rested some starters in the second half of the meaningless season finale and Washington lost a 19-7 lead and the game to Philadelphia.

No matter. The Redskins entered the playoffs rested from a week off and prepared to terrorize the opposition.

"We had the frame of mind that we couldn't be stopped unless we beat ourselves," said Redskins offensive lineman Raleigh McKenzie.

Added Rypien, "We thought we were pretty much unbeatable, but if you lose in the playoffs, no one remembers how good your regular season is."

This time Washington's second season was going to be even better than its first.

Atlanta, always a cocky team, was flying even higher after upsetting New Orleans in the first round.

Coach Jerry Glanville's Falcons, who had lost 56-17 at RFK just two months before, bragged about what they were going to do in the rematch even though they were 0-7 at RFK.

"Glanville's arrogance had us fired up," Mann said. "You don't do the kind of talking he does and never set foot on the field."

It didn't help Glanville's cause when he and star cornerback Deion Sanders filmed a video on the field before the game. Or that they had rapper Hammer and boxer Evander Holyfield in their entourage.

"It's like they all want to be movie stars," Mitchell said. "The problem is you still have to go play the game. You have to go out and just be a football team and we were better."

Maybe Glanville knew that when he hoisted a Redskins helmet during warmups.

"You're thinking, 'This guy is a lunatic,' " Jacoby said. "Coming into this place against this team that's been on a tear the whole year and doing this. . . . That's a motivating factor."

So was living up to the legacy of Washington's previous champions.

"Before the game, guys were holding up their Super Bowl rings in the locker room," Rypien remembered. "Some guys were on their last legs, but they had a lot of leg left."

Then there was the weather. Gibbs never used the elements as an excuse. In fact, the coach hammered home the idea to his players that bad weather was to their advantage.

"Bad weather. Cold weather. Rainy weather. What kind of weather is it? Redskins weather," Monk recited from memory with a smile.

If that was the case, it was surely Redskins weather that afternoon. It began raining the night before and it didn't stop for days. What's more the winds whipped around the stadium at 30 miles per hour.

"We're basically a running team that can pass," said Bostic, who said he had never played in worse conditions in 16 years in college and the pros. "They're a passing team. It was advantage, Redskins."

Glanville switched his blitzing, man-to-man defense to zone, but it was impossible for Atlanta to redo its offensive gameplan. The Falcons' "Red Gun" run-and-shoot was built for speed not for mud.

"A run-and-shoot in weather like this is like a gun with one bullet," lamented Deion Sanders.

The Falcons hung in there for a while with their one bullet. The Redskins had cut back on their deep passing game too and managed just 50 yards on their first three possessions. But late in the first quarter, Washington began an 11-play, 81-yard march. Rypien's 19-yard pass to Clark on third down from the Atlanta 31 got the Redskins close. Two plays later, the quarterback called a draw off an audible. Rookie halfback Ricky Ervins, not as used to the poor footing as veterans Byner and Riggs, ran 17 yards to the end zone through a huge hole opened by fine blocks by Lachey and Monk.

"You learn about people in weather like this," Bostic said of Ervins, who would gain 104 yards. "Ricky showed he was a mud back."

Three plays later Mann forced a fumble which defensive tackle Jumpy Geathers recovered at the Atlanta 39. Ricky Sanders beat Deion Sanders on a 26-yard slant to set up ex-Falcon Riggs spiking the ball in the end zone. Washington led 14-0 after scoring two touchdowns in 3:11.

Cornerback Martin Mayhew and linebacker Kurt Gouveia ended Atlanta's next two series with interceptions. The only reason the Falcons — who didn't make a first down on six straight possessions — were still in the game was that Lohmiller had missed three field goal tries in the mud. After the last failure, quarterback Chris Miller did move Atlanta 80 yards for a touchdown with a big assist from Mayhew's pass interference penalty which negated Green's pickoff.

It was just 14-7 at halftime and Glanville said, "We thought we had a chance. We thought we were sitting right where we wanted to."

Instead, the Falcons went backwards on their first series. Mitchell returned the punt 26 yards to the Atlanta 18. Lohmiller's subsequent 24-yard field goal increased the margin to 10 points. When Atlanta's Norm Johnson missed his 45-yarder on the next drive, the Falcons were heading for their gold chains and rap music. The Redskins were heading for the NFC Championship Game against Detroit.

Washington defensive coordinator Richie Petitbon had figured the way to beat the run-and-shoot wasn't to load up on defensive backs but to focus on the run and rely on his usual zone to defend the pass. Especially in the mud. Atlanta gained 150 yards in the air — just 20 fewer than Washington — but the longest completion went for 17 yards and the Falcons were outgained 162-43 on the ground.

"They had the field covered," Miller said of Washington's defense.

"Our coaches had a great gameplan," Gouveia said. "They put us in a position to succeed."

And to force six turnovers.

"Our defense kept giving us chances like they have all season," Gibbs said afterwards.

When Riggs' second touchdown followed Marshall's fumble recovery with 6:32 left, it began raining . . . yellow seat cushions as the fans spontaneously tossed their souvenirs onto the field.

"It was amazing to see thousands of seat cushions coming from everywhere," Orr said. "I don't know if there were any left in the stands. It was amazing how long they kept coming. It wasn't a five-second thing. It went on and on and on."

Jacoby, not an emotional sort, also treasures that moment.

"I had a big, old smile on my face, sitting on my butt on the goal line and Gerald is behind me [in the end zone] and all of a sudden I look up and see those yellow things flying down," Jacoby said. "It was a great feeling. The fans rubbed it back in Glanville's face."

Glanville didn't bother to shake Gibbs' hand afterwards, but at least he didn't make excuses.

"We didn't get beat by the rain," said Glanville. "We got beat by the Redskins."

And in 1991, that was no disgrace. Washington would go on to crush Detroit 41-10 for the NFC title and beat Buffalo 37-24 in a Super Bowl that wasn't even that close.

MARK RYPIEN

Mark Rypien

No Redskin had more of a rollercoaster career than Mark Rypien. Stashed on injured reserve by coach Joe Gibbs during his first two years, Rypien was the Super Bowl XXVI Most Valuable Player as he quarterbacked Washington to the title during his third year as a starter. Two years later, Rypien was gone, a victim of his injury-related decline and an organizational shakeup.

Rypien didn't have the arm of Sonny Jurgensen or Doug Williams or the fiery personality of Billy Kilmer or Joe Theismann. The slow-footed Rypien wasn't a great athlete. But Rypien was a fierce competitor and he understood the game, specifically Gibbs' offense.

"Those two years I sat out, I questioned whether I would ever be able to play in this league," Rypien said. "I was a sixth-round guy [from Washington State]. People didn't have real high expectations for me. If I had been in another system, I don't know how I would have done."

We'll never know, but Rypien, who was a backup in Cleveland and St. Louis after leaving Washington, was a winner with the Redskins. During his six seasons as the starter, the Redskins were 50-29 with Rypien, 9-15 with another quarterback at the helm. Rypien believes he would still be in Washington if Gibbs hadn't retired in 1993.

"Ryp was one of the brightest guys I ever coached," Gibbs said. "He looked a little clumsy because he was so big [6-foot-4, 234 pounds]. I don't think people really gave him his due. If you got something open deep, Ryp would hit it. He was a great deep thrower."

Said defensive end Charles Mann, "No one ever understood what coach Gibbs wanted better than Mark did. After a while, Mark even talked like him. Mark was coach Gibbs' greatest creation."

The coach-student relationship was first displayed on Sept. 25, 1988 at Phoenix. Rypien had become Williams' backup following the trade of the disgruntled Jay Schroeder to the Los Angeles Raiders. Williams came down with appendicitis and Gibbs turned to Rypien, who responded with 303 yards and three touchdowns. However, the defending Super Bowl champions were stunned by the Cardinals 30-21. Rypien was even better the next week, passing for 382 yards and two touchdowns, but the New York Giants edged Washington, 24-23. Despite his solid statistics, the Redskins only split Rypien's first 14 starts and after he tossed three interceptions in a rout by the Raiders in 1989, Gibbs benched him.

"I learned from the situation with Jay and Doug," Rypien said. "If things aren't going your way, you can go home and tell your wife you feel cheated, but you can't pout in public. And I learned from Doug that you have to operate on an even keel. You can't get too excited when things are going well or too low when they're not."

When the offense generated just 13 points in two games with the creaking Williams, it was Rypien's job again. Washington won five of its last six games, just missing the playoffs. Rypien led the Redskins to the second round in 1990 and then to the mountaintop in 1991.

Rypien, who also guided Washington to the second round in 1992, is proud to be the only Redskins quarterback to win a Super Bowl in a non-strike season. But he credits much of his 1991 stardom to his wonderful supporting cast – which allowed him to be sacked just nine times – and the veteran coaching staff.

However, Rypien may be too humble.

"What we did on offense we couldn't have done without Mark," said tight end Terry Orr. "He was just so smart. Joe put all the pressure on him because he knew the offense so well."

Typically, the game Rypien remembers most fondly isn't his record-tying 442-yard, six-touchdown performance against Atlanta in 1991. It was a 15-13 victory the next year in Minnesota, a game in which he passed for just 148 yards and didn't reach the end zone.

"We were banged up [offensive linemen Jim Lachey and Jeff Bostic were out and Joe Jacoby and Mark Schlereth were ailing] and they came at us with everything," Rypien said. "I was getting knocked around on almost every play, but we hung in there and pulled it out [on Chip Lohmiller's last-minute field goal]. Those are the games you're proudest of, the ones when you overcome adversity."

Rypien, who hoped to play an 11th NFL season in 1996 at age 34, certainly faced his share of adversity during his time in Washington. But he learned from Williams and took the highs and lows in stride.

"Mark was the greatest guy when he was breaking in and he was the same guy when he was going out," Mann said. "He never changed."

photo by Arnie Sachs and the staff of Consolidated News Photo
BRIAN MITCHELL

Brian Mitchell

Brian Mitchell is a closet linebacker. Oh, he may be a record-setting kick and punt returner, good running back and even an emergency quarterback, but the man lives to hit people.

Hit people? Isn't he on the wrong side of the ball? Mitchell lifted weights with linebackers to become a gigantic returner at 220 pounds — about 40 pounds more than usual. He learned it's better to hit opponents hard so they aren't so eager to try him again.

"I have a linebacker's mentality," said Mitchell, who also makes his share of tackles covering kicks. "When [opponents] tackle me they feel the pain because I'm not coming at them soft. I go into the game thinking somebody is going to have to pay."

Away from the football field, Mitchell is a nice guy who loves to cook Cajun food from his native Louisiana. But from inside his helmet, Mitchell loves to talk trash during the game. He disrespectfully tosses the football at tacklers after the play, and taunts opponents who kick away from him.

Opponents got mad, and sometimes they got even. In 1994, Mitchell set an NFL record for most combined kickoff and punt return yardage (1,930), but wasn't voted to the Pro Bowl. However, he earned a 1995 trip to Hawaii despite slightly lower numbers.

"You're supposed to be the best at your position," Mitchell said, "and I think I was the best for the three or four years I didn't make it. If they don't like how I play on the field, that's their problem. It's a game of emotion and who has the strongest mind. A lot of guys can't handle that."

But Mitchell really gets mad when opponents kick away from him. After a 59-yard touchdown punt return and kickoff returns of 44 and 42 yards against the Philadelphia Eagles on Oct. 8, 1995, the Eagles' punter aimed toward the sidelines rather than test Mitchell.

"I don't respect them at all," he said. "We're in the NFL and if you're going to kick the ball out of bounds you're not being a professional. It may help them, but it doesn't look good. Fans don't come to see you kick the ball in the stands. You play inside the lines, not outside."

Against the Denver Broncos on Sept. 17, 1995, Mitchell produced a club record 290 combined yards, including a 36-yard touchdown run, a 52-yard punt return and 188 yards on six kickoff returns.

"You see Michael Jordan get into a zone, and sometimes I think I get into a zone," Mitchell said. "No one is going to stop me."

But Mitchell dislikes being called a kick returner. At Southwest Louisiana, he was the first player ever to throw for more than 5,000 yards and rush for more than 3,000 yards. He also set an NCAA record for quarterbacks with 47 rushing touchdowns. Mitchell still wonders what might have happened if he had chosen to play quarterback in the Canadian Football League, though his days of yearning to throw have finally passed.

Although he was good enough to be the starting halfback — rushing for 116 yards in the 1993 opener against the Dallas Cowboys — Mitchell has become the Redskins' third-down runner. He was also the team's second-leading receiver in 1995 with 38 catches. Mitchell once worried over his multiple roles, but no longer.

"I don't know [which position I prefer] because I've never been one to limit myself," he said. "I'm a football player, not a kick returner or a running back."

Mitchell may not have even peaked at age 28. If he leads the NFL in all-purpose yardage in 1996, he'll join Hall of Famers Gale Sayers and Jim Brown as the only players to do so three straight years. Special teams coach Pete Rodriguez said, "Brian is just approaching his peak. I expect another three, four years out of him. Brian is one of the best returners in the NFL. He has great quickness, excellent instincts and tremendous toughness."

Three or four more years? That's plenty of time for more touchdowns, taunts and tackles.

As A Redskin

Position: Kick/punt returner, running back.

Years: 1990 - present.

Stats: 5,004 kick return yards, 1,938 punt return yards, 1,023 yards rushing, 89 receptions, 11 touchdowns.

Greatest season: Set NFL record for most combined punt and kickoff return yardage with 1,930 in 1994. His 1,478 kickoff return yards were the second most in NFL history. Set team record with 2,477 all-purpose yards while leading NFL with 14.1 yard punt return average.

Honors: Pro Bowl, 1995.

Today: Active player with Redskins.

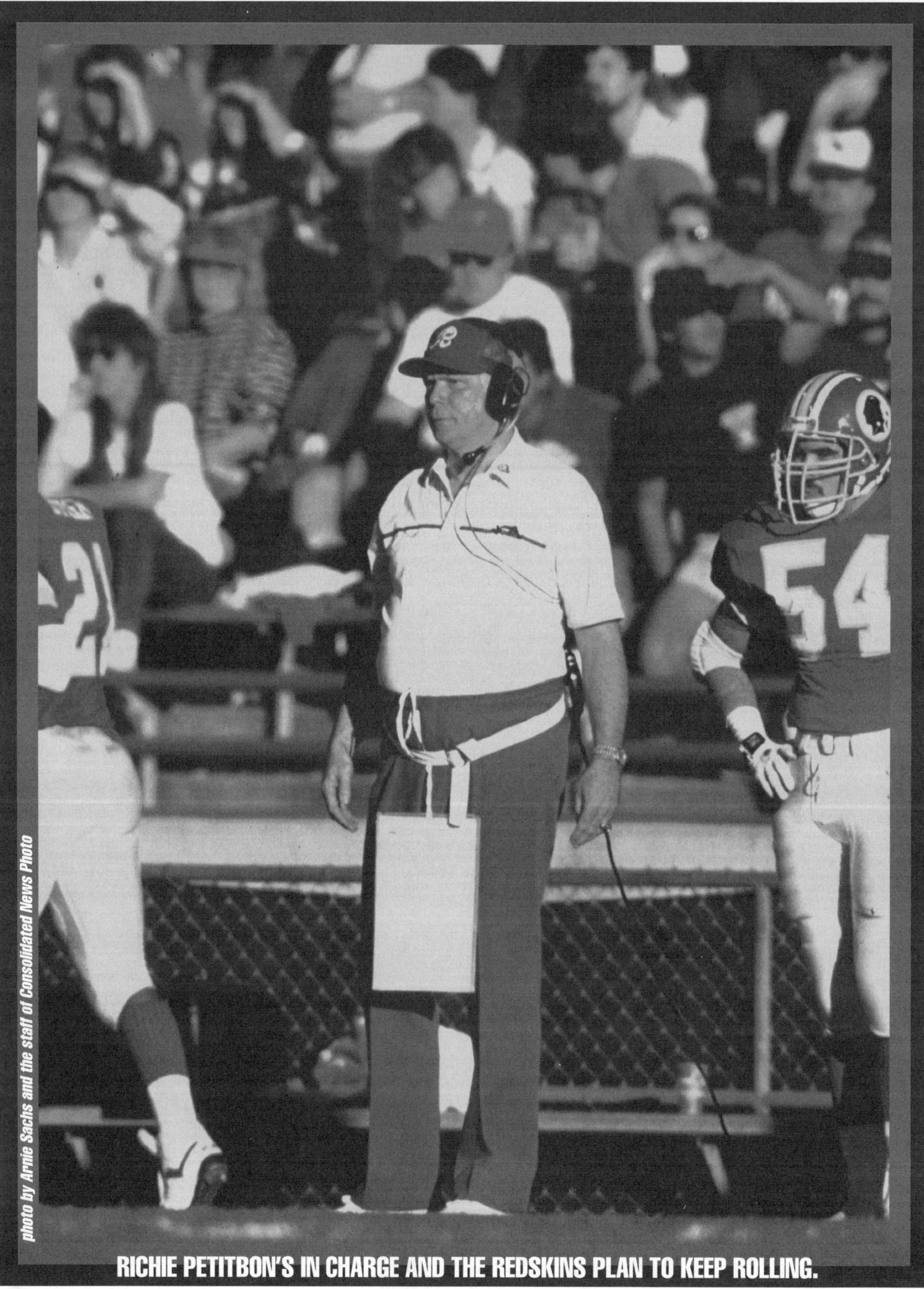

RICHIE PETITBON'S IN CHARGE AND THE REDSKINS PLAN TO KEEP ROLLING.

End of an Era

Redskins 35, Cowboys 16

The man who crafted three Super Bowl champions had departed in March, taking a chunk of the Redskins' glory days with him. A huge chunk. For a dozen years, Washington felt secure in Joe Gibbs. And it felt confident. By the time he was finished, it wasn't just enough to win. The Redskins had to win big.

Yet, when 1993 opened, the Redskins remained confident. Richie was in charge. Everything would be the same.

"That was a shock," cornerback Darrell Green said of Gibbs' March 5 retirement. That same day, defensive coordinator Richie Petitbon was handed the job. "But when [Petitbon] came in, that seemed natural to me."

And to everyone else.

"The big thing was, we were still the Redskins," said offensive lineman Raleigh McKenzie. "We were still the guys who had won the championship [two years] before. We lost a great guy in Joe Gibbs. But we've got Richie. He said, 'We're not going to change the oil we've been using in the engine. We'll just keep on going.'"

In many ways, Petitbon, hired by coach Jack Pardee in 1978, was Gibbs' opposite. Gibbs thrived on long hours, sleeping overnight in his office. Petitbon got his work done by early evening. Petitbon was a gambler, confounding teams with timely blitzes. Gibbs preferred a conservative attack. Gibbs was a born-again Christian; Petitbon as a safety was a partying member of Washington's "Over the Hill Gang" in the 1970s.

But like Gibbs, Petitbon had earned the players' respect, impressing them with halftime adjustments. Many times the Redskins pounded teams in the second half, beating opponents with different tactics. Especially in the 1991 season when they won the Super Bowl.

Other teams noticed. Indianapolis, Tampa Bay, New England and Denver sought interviews with Petitbon at various times, but he turned them down. Chicago (where he had played) and New Orleans (where he grew up), among others, considered him a finalist for head coaching vacancies. Those jobs went to Dave Wannstedt and Jim Mora, respectively, and Petitbon remained a Redskin.

When Gibbs left, the club considered itself lucky Petitbon was still around. And he was happy to still be in Washington.

"To see this job go to someone else would have been a disaster," said Petitbon, the only member of the organization to have played or coached in every Redskins Super Bowl appearance. "[But] let's face it. Time was running out for me."

Those who played on Petitbon's defense swore by the man. To Green, Petitbon was a surrogate father. It was a relationship constructed through battles, sometimes with one another. When Green was a rookie, he once ran off the field and all he heard was Petitbon's voice exploding with expletives.

"I wasn't used to that," Green said. "And I'm like, Man! So I'm hollering back at him. I wasn't cursing, just yelling: 'Don't you talk to me like that!' It was in the heat of the game. I remember that Monday he called me in and said, 'Look, babe, this is not personal.'"

But their relationship became personal. Green compared Petitbon to the father who is tough on his kids, but when those kids are thrust into real-life situations, they survive because of the hard-learned lessons.

For 11 years, Green and Petitbon co-existed. As Green grew and his family expanded, conversations centered around subjects other than football.

"He was someone I'd go to bat for," Green said.

In the minicamp after Petitbon replaced Gibbs, Green had a sore leg and figured it was wise to hold back.

"I hadn't done any training at all so I said, 'Look coach, I'm not going to run the 40 [yard dash],'" Green said. "He said, 'No, go out there and run it because I want the ship to look smooth. Limp, hobble. I want 100

	1	2	3	4	Total
REDSKINS 35, COWBOYS 16					
Cowboys	6	0	7	3	16
Redskins	0	14	7	14	35

FIRST QUARTER
D — Irvin 80 pass from Aikman (kick failed), D 6-0

SECOND QUARTER
W — Sanders 15 pass from Rypien (Lohmiller kick), W 7-6
W — Mitchell 1 run (Lohmiller kick), W 14-6

THIRD QUARTER
W — Middleton 1 pass from Rypien (Lohmiller kick), W 21-6
D — Harper 33 pass from Aikman (Elliott kick), W 21-13

FOURTH QUARTER
W — Monk 15 pass from Rypien (Lohmiller kick), W 28-13
D — Elliott 22 FG, W 28-16
W — Mitchell 29 run (Lohmiller kick), W 35-16

percent participation.' I said, 'That's all you've got to say to me.' That was an honor to me. He had asked me to do this."

That summer, Washington finished 3-1 in the pre-season and energized the town with a 41-10 exhibition-opening win at home over Cleveland. However, that same night, offensive left tackle Jim Lachey tore the anterior cruciate ligament in his right knee and was lost for the season. But Mo Elewonibi had filled in the year before and played well. Why couldn't he do it again?

So when defending Super Bowl champion Dallas arrived for the Monday Night game in the season opener, everyone figured it was status quo. Joe. Richie. Doesn't matter. It's the Redskins.

And, the players had something to prove. The year before, they had been 9-7 and only a late fourth-quarter fumble by quarterback Mark Rypien cost them an upset bid at San Francisco in the NFC Divisional Playoffs. And the Redskins had won the Super Bowl in 1991.

But, in the opener, a prime motivation for most was Petitbon.

"If you ever wanted something real badly, it was that opening game against Dallas," said defensive end Charles Mann. "We didn't want it for ourselves so much. We wanted it for Richie. This was an opportunity for us to affirm the signing of Richie Petitbon as our coach, a player's coach, a good guy. We wanted to show the world that the Redskins were still there. How do we show it? By going out there and thrashing the Cowboys.

"Everybody was extremely focused. We just systematically whipped their behinds. We went crazy in the locker room. We knocked them off their high horse. People say they didn't have Emmitt [Smith, the all-Pro halfback who was holding out]. We knew there was going to be a blemish on that win. We didn't want any blemishes for Richie."

That wasn't a problem. After all, Smith (whose replacement, Derrick Lassic, rushed for 75 yards on 16 carries) didn't play defense. And the Dallas defense — which included end Charles Haley, linebacker Ken Norton, defensive tackle Russell Maryland and safety Darren Woodson — couldn't stop the Redskins' offense.

Washington's ground game chewed them up, grinding out four drives of 65 yards or more.

"We were playing the world champs and it was a great showcase for us," Petitbon said. "We were very, very confident going in. We knew what [the Cowboys] wanted to try and do and we thought we'd be able to run the football on them. The game went about the way we thought it would go."

It didn't go their way early, even though safety Pat Eilers recovered a fumbled punt on the Dallas 16. However, Chip Lohmiller missed a 32-yard field-goal attempt. Four plays later, Dallas quarterback Troy Aikman capitalized on a miscommunication between cornerback A.J. Johnson and safety Danny Copeland to hit a wide-open Michael Irvin for an 80-yard score. Lin Elliott missed the extra point attempt.

That was the extent of Dallas' first-half highlights. Washington's domination was about to begin.

A 13-play, 80-yard drive that lasted 7:15 ended with a 15-yard Rypien to Ricky Sanders touchdown pass. Rookie running back Reggie Brooks, a second-round pick, gained 48 yards on eight carries on that drive. Also in that series, offensive coordinator Rod Dowhower scrapped his two-back, one tight end look and returned to the two tight-end schemes of the Gibbs days.

"We were concerned about Rod running the offense," receiver Art Monk said. "But he called a great game."

The second touchdown followed a bad punt by Washington's Kelly Goodburn. But it hit Dallas' James Washington and Eilers again recovered at the Cowboys' 17. Four plays later Brian Mitchell, making his first start at running back, swept in from the 1-yard line with 40 seconds left in the half.

Nothing changed after halftime. On Washington's first second-half possession, a 78-yard drive resulted in another touchdown, a 1-yard scoring pass from Rypien to tight end Rod Middleton.

Dallas answered with an 80-yard scoring drive on five plays — four of them Aikman completions. That touchdown only preceded the Redskins' top effort of the evening. Ironically, it began when Mitchell downed a kickoff. At the 1-yard line.

"I felt two inches tall," he said.

But 99 yards later — after Rypien's 15-yard touchdown pass to Monk — Mitchell felt much better. The 13-play, seven-minute march made it 28-13 and sucked the life out of Dallas.

"That's what your good linemen feast on," said center Jeff Bostic. "When you run the football and they know you're running the football and they can't stop it."

All that remained was the final quarter, which proved to be a formality. No way would Washington blow this game, not when the Redskins felt they had so much to prove. They showed to the 56,813 at RFK and to world that Petitbon deserved this opportunity and that they could once more make a run at the Super Bowl.

Rypien completed 22-of-34 passes for 161 yards and three touchdowns; Mitchell rushed for 116 yards on 23 carries and scored the game's final touchdown on a 29-yard run late in the fourth quarter. Mitchell had erased his own doubts about his ability to be a starter. Sanders caught five passes for 40 yards while Monk grabbed three for 58. And Elewonibi shut down Haley. The Cowboys helped with four fumbles — just five fewer than they had the previous season.

Dallas certainly couldn't stop Washington's running game. The Redskins rushed for 171 yards — 80 more than the Cowboys and controlled the ball for 35:03. Brooks flashed his potential, gaining 53 yards on 11 carries.

"They basically kicked our butts on the front line," said Dallas safety Bill Bates.

As for Smith's absence, Aikman said, "Emmitt doesn't run patterns for us. He doesn't play defense for us."

All was right in the Redskins' world.

"We weren't surprised we beat them, just how easy it was," Rypien recalled. "They didn't have Emmitt, but we had lost coach Gibbs. We didn't have any doubt that we were still a top team. That was one of the most satisfying games I've ever played in with the way the season had ended the year before."

Bostic said, "Everyone was stoked [after the game]. That was a physical thumping. It's not like the game was that close. It was a physical mashing."

McKenzie agreed.

"It was one of those games you beg for," he said. "You'd like to have 16 of them during the year."

They didn't. In fact, it was the last game of its kind for Washington in 1993. Everyone has theories as to what happened, the simplest and most common being injuries. Only four players (Green, linebacker Kurt Gouveia, safety Brad Edwards and Middleton) started every game.

After Lachey, the next big injury came in Week 2 when Rypien partially tore a ligament in his knee in a loss to Arizona, the first in a string of six straight defeats. Bostic and Jacoby battled injuries all season. Mann hurt his knee. Eventually, the losses piled up and rumors of Petitbon's future circulated.

Three days after the 4-12 season ended with a loss to Minnesota, Petitbon was fired by owner Jack Kent Cooke.

By the following season, Rypien, Monk, Mann, Sanders, Bostic and Jacoby were gone.

"The last hurrah was in the struggle of the year," Green said. "We were together. We were like a bunch of old soldiers hanging out, everyone's on crutches waiting to go home."

The victory over Dallas wasn't the continuation of the most successful phase in Redskins' history.

Instead, as Mitchell said, "We were at the end of an era."

Mark Rypien and the Redskins would crash after the big opening win.

About The Authors

John Keim is an award-winning sportswriter for the Journal Newspapers in suburban Washington, D.C. for whom he has covered the Redskins since 1994. He has also written about the Redskins for Joe Theismann's Pro Football Yearbook, and Redskin Review. The Ohio State graduate and Lakewood, Ohio native resides in Chantilly, Va., with his wife Kerry and son Matthew.

David Elfin has covered the Washington Redskins for five seasons for the Washington Times. Elfin, a native Washingtonian, is a graduate of the University of Pennsylvania and Syracuse University's Newhouse School. He has won numerous awards during his 14-year sportswriting career and serves on the board of directors of the Professional Football Writers of America. Elfin lives in Bethesda, Md., with his wife Loretta and daughters Julie and Amy.

Rick Snider covers the Washington Redskins for the Washington Times. An award-winning sportswriter for 18 years, the native Washingtonian has also authored "Twenty Unforgettable Horse Races" and "Channel Surfing in the '90s: In Search of the Remote Control, Classic Rock and Mini Vans" and co-written "Stop If They're Throwing Rocks: Coaching Baseball For All Ages." The University of Maryland graduate is president of 21st Century Online Publishing Inc., an Internet-based publishing company. Snider lives in Waldorf, Md., with his wife Lisa and daughters Megan and Katelyn.